PAT BROWN, MBA

TennisMoney101

Using Tennis to Teach the Basics of Money

ABRAM · 47 · BROWN

First published by AbramBrown47 2026

First edition

ISBN: 978-1-967737-55-0

This book was professionally typeset on Reedsy.
Find out more at reedsy.com

Contents

Foreword

Tennis teaches you patience in a way few sports can.

There is no clock to save you. No teammate to bail you out. No shortcut to the end of the match. Every point must be earned, and momentum can turn on a single mistake or a single moment of discipline. You learn quickly that talent alone is not enough. Conditioning matters. Preparation matters. Shot selection matters. Most of all, consistency matters.

Money works the same way.

Many athletes leave tennis believing they will finally have more freedom once the matches stop. More time. More flexibility. More control. What they often discover instead is uncertainty. Without a coach setting the schedule, without daily practices and clear performance metrics, financial decisions feel abstract and confusing. The rules are unclear. The feedback is delayed. Mistakes do not show up immediately, but they compound quietly over time.

That gap between discipline on the court and discipline with money is where many athletes struggle.

This book exists to close that gap.

Tennis Money 101 is not about turning athletes into economists or stock pickers. It is about translating a mindset you already have into a new arena. If you have trained for years, adjusted your game under pressure, studied film, and competed through adversity, you already understand the core principles required for long term financial success. You just have not been shown how those principles apply to money.

In tennis, you do not try to hit a winner on every shot. You build points. You move your opponent. You wait for the right opportunity. You accept that some days you win ugly and some days you lose despite playing well.

You trust the process because you understand the season is longer than one match.

Financial success follows the same pattern.

You will not win every month. Markets will fluctuate. Income will change. Life will throw distractions and pressure points your way. The athletes who succeed financially are not the ones who chase hot streaks or panic after a bad set. They are the ones who stay disciplined, manage risk, and keep showing up point after point.

This book speaks directly to that athlete.

It assumes you know what it feels like to grind through long rallies, to stay composed after a double fault, and to reset after losing a tough game. It assumes you respect fundamentals even when they are boring. It assumes you understand that preparation done when nobody is watching is what shows up when it matters most.

Each section of this book uses tennis as the lens for understanding money. Budgeting becomes reducing unforced errors. Investing becomes constructing points instead of chasing highlights. Asset allocation becomes court positioning. Risk management becomes shot selection under pressure. Retirement planning becomes winning the match over time, not just the first set.

The goal is not perfection. The goal is control.

Control over your decisions. Control over your reactions. Control over your future options.

You do not need to be wealthy to benefit from this book. You do not need a financial background. You do not need to have everything figured out. You only need a willingness to apply the same discipline you brought to tennis to a different part of your life.

Tennis rewards players who think long term. Players who understand that winning one point does not guarantee winning the match, but losing focus on a single point can cost it. Money rewards the same mindset.

If you commit to learning the fundamentals, staying patient, and trusting the process, the results will follow. Not overnight. Not without setbacks. But steadily, deliberately, and sustainably.

That is how matches are won.
That is how financial independence is built.
One point at a time.

Introduction

Every tennis player learns this lesson early, whether a coach says it out loud or not.

You do not win a match by thinking about the final score. You win it by playing the point in front of you. If you get caught up thinking about the trophy, the ranking, or the handshake at the net, your footwork slips, your timing goes, and unforced errors creep in. The best players reset after every point. They accept what just happened, good or bad, and focus on the next ball.

Money works the same way.

Most people lose financially not because they lack intelligence, but because they think in extremes. They want the big win. The perfect investment. The moment where everything clicks at once. When that does not happen quickly, frustration sets in. Discipline fades. Shortcuts become tempting.

Tennis teaches you that there are no shortcuts.

You build a match one rally at a time. You manage energy. You choose high percentage shots. You adjust when momentum shifts. You stay patient when nothing seems to be working. Financial success is built the same way. It is not about one big decision. It is about hundreds of small, boring, disciplined decisions made consistently over time.

After tennis, this can feel unfamiliar.

For most of your athletic life, improvement was visible. Rankings moved. Match results were clear. Coaches gave feedback. Training blocks had structure. When the uniform comes off, that structure disappears. Money decisions do not come with instant feedback. You can overspend, delay saving, or make a poor investment choice and feel fine for months or years. The consequences show up later, quietly, when options are limited.

That delay is what makes money feel confusing.

In tennis, you respect fundamentals because you have seen what happens when you abandon them. In finance, many athletes never get that early lesson. They are told to save, invest, or be responsible, but no one explains how those actions connect to long term outcomes. Without context, money feels abstract and intimidating.

This book is designed to slow the game down.

Tennis is a sport of patterns. Crosscourt rallies. High margin targets. Depth before pace. You do not play every opponent the same way, but the fundamentals do not change. Financial principles work the same way. Markets change. Rules evolve. Personal situations differ. The underlying disciplines remain constant.

You win matches by reducing unforced errors.

You build wealth the same way.

You win matches by managing momentum.

You manage money the same way.

You win matches by trusting preparation under pressure.

You succeed financially the same way.

This book is not asking you to become obsessed with money. It is asking you to approach it the way you approached tennis when you were at your best. With intention. With patience. With awareness.

Some points will be lost. Some financial decisions will not work out the way you hoped. That does not mean the strategy is wrong. In tennis, you do not abandon your game plan because you lost a tough game. You adjust, recommit, and keep competing. Financially, the same mindset separates those who stay steady from those who spiral.

You will see the same themes repeated throughout this book because repetition matters. Just like drills. Just like footwork. Just like match play. Concepts stick when they are revisited from different angles and applied in different situations.

This is not a book about becoming rich overnight.

It is a book about building control over your future.

Control over your cash flow.

Control over your decisions.

Control over your response to pressure.

Financial independence is not a finish line you sprint through. It is a long match played over decades. You win it by showing up prepared, minimizing mistakes, and staying disciplined when emotions run high.

If you commit to winning one point at a time with your money, the match takes care of itself.

That is the mindset this book is built on.

Now it is time to step onto the court.

About This Book

Tennis is a sport built on habits, not moments.

From the outside, people see the winners, the aces, the highlight passing shots. What they do not see are the thousands of reps that make those shots possible. The footwork drills. The boring rally patterns. The discipline to hit the same shot again and again until it becomes automatic. Tennis players understand that matches are rarely won by flash alone. They are won by consistency, preparation, and decision making under pressure.

Money works the same way.

This book exists because too many athletes leave tennis with a world class understanding of discipline and a limited understanding of how to apply it financially. They know how to train. They know how to compete. They know how to handle pressure. What they were rarely taught is how those same skills translate into managing income, saving, investing, and planning for life beyond the court.

Tennis Money 101 bridges that gap.

The purpose of this book is not to overwhelm you with technical detail or turn you into a financial expert. It is to reframe money using a language and structure you already understand. If you have trained through early mornings, managed nerves on big points, and trusted your game plan when momentum shifted, you already have the mindset needed to make strong financial decisions.

Tennis teaches patience.

Money demands it.

Tennis teaches you to play percentages.

Money rewards the same thinking.

Tennis teaches you to accept short term losses in service of long term wins.

Money works the same way.

Throughout this book, tennis is used as the primary analogy for every major financial concept. Budgeting is framed as reducing unforced errors. Saving is about building endurance. Investing is about constructing points rather than going for winners too early. Risk management becomes shot selection. Asset allocation becomes court positioning. Rebalancing mirrors momentum shifts during a match.

These comparisons are not gimmicks. They exist because the mental skills that make someone a strong tennis player are the same skills that create financial stability over time.

One of the biggest challenges athletes face with money is delayed feedback. In tennis, you know immediately when a shot misses. In finance, mistakes often feel invisible at first. Overspending does not hurt right away. Skipping savings feels harmless early on. Chasing a hot investment might even feel rewarding in the short term. The consequences show up later, when options are fewer and pressure is higher.

Tennis players understand delayed payoff better than most people.

You train for months for a match that lasts hours. You build fitness long before it shows up on the scoreboard. You trust the process even when results lag behind effort. This book applies that same long view to money. It emphasizes systems over shortcuts, discipline over excitement, and preparation over prediction.

This is also a book about control.

In tennis, you cannot control the opponent, the wind, or the officiating. You can control your preparation, your effort, and your shot selection. Financially, you cannot control markets, tax law changes, or economic cycles. You can control your behavior, your planning, and your consistency. This book focuses relentlessly on the controllables.

It also respects that every athlete's situation is different.

Some readers are current student athletes. Some are former competitive players building careers. Some may experience sudden income or financial opportunity. Others are starting slowly. The principles in this book apply across those differences because they are rooted in fundamentals, not circumstances.

You do not need to read this book in one sitting.

You do not need to master everything at once.

Like tennis, progress comes from repetition. You will see familiar themes reappear because they matter. You will be reminded to slow down when emotions rise. You will be encouraged to play the long game even when short term temptation is strong.

This book assumes you respect coaching.

It assumes you respect structure.

It assumes you are willing to compete for your future.

Tennis does not reward impatience.

Neither does money.

If you approach your finances the way you approached your best seasons on the court, with focus, discipline, and trust in the process, the results will compound over time.

That is what this book is here to teach.

Not how to win quickly.

But how to win consistently.

One point at a time.

Foolish Assumptions

Every good coach starts with assumptions.

Not because they believe everyone is the same, but because clarity matters. If expectations are not set early, confusion shows up later. This section does the same thing. It lays out what this book assumes about you, not to judge you, but to meet you where you actually are.

Some of these assumptions will fit perfectly. Some may challenge you. That is intentional.

Assumption One: You Understand Discipline, Even If You Are Not Using It Financially Yet

This book assumes you know what discipline feels like.

You have shown up early. You have trained when motivation was low. You have repeated boring drills until they mattered. You may not currently apply that same structure to money, but the muscle exists.

If you can commit to daily footwork, you can commit to consistent saving.

If you can follow a match plan, you can follow a financial plan.

The gap is not ability. It is translation.

Assumption Two: You Have Never Been Properly Taught This

This book assumes no one sat you down and clearly explained money in a way that made sense.

You likely heard advice. Save more. Do not spend too much. Invest early. Avoid debt. None of that is wrong. It is just incomplete. Without context, advice feels abstract and easy to ignore.

In tennis, telling someone to "hit better" is useless. You break it down into grip, footwork, spacing, and timing. Money deserves the same breakdown. This book assumes you were never given that level of instruction.

Assumption Three: You Think in Points, Not in Years

Athletes are trained to focus on the next rep, the next drill, the next match. Long term thinking exists, but it is built through daily execution.

This book assumes you respond better to systems than to lectures about retirement thirty years from now. It frames money in points, games, and sets because that is how progress actually happens.

Financial success is not a single event. It is a long match won through consistent execution.

Assumption Four: You Respect Coaching and Structure

This book assumes you respect structure, even if you resist authority.

You understand the value of a plan.

You understand the cost of freelancing.

You understand that fundamentals win when pressure rises.

Money without structure turns emotional quickly. This book is built like a training plan, not a motivational speech. If you want hype, this is not the right book. If you want a framework you can execute, it is.

Assumption Five: You Have Felt Pressure and Responded to It

Tennis exposes you.

There is no hiding during a long rally or a tight tiebreak. You have felt nerves. You have made mistakes under pressure. You have also stayed composed and executed when it mattered.

This book assumes you know what pressure feels like and that you want tools to manage it better financially. Markets create pressure. Life creates pressure. Money decisions amplify both. The skills you used on court apply directly here.

Assumption Six: You Want Control More Than Flash

This book assumes you want control over your future, not just excitement.

Control over your cash flow.

Control over your options.

Control over how much pressure money creates in your life.

Flashy financial stories exist everywhere. They rarely last. Tennis players know that winners look great but consistency wins matches. This book assumes you are willing to trade excitement for reliability.

Assumption Seven: You Are Willing to Be Honest With Yourself

Finally, this book assumes you are willing to look at your habits without excuses.

In tennis, film does not lie. In money, statements do not lie either. Progress starts with awareness. This book will ask you to slow down, assess reality, and make adjustments without judgment.

That takes maturity.

If any of these assumptions feel uncomfortable, that is a good sign. Growth usually does.

This book is not here to impress you.

It is here to help you execute.

If you bring the same honesty, discipline, and patience to your finances that you once brought to the court, you will be fine.

That is the core belief behind every page that follows.

How This Playbook Is Organized

Tennis players do not train randomly.

There is a progression. Footwork before shot selection. Consistency before power. Defense before offense. You build a base, then layer complexity. You do not jump straight into match play without drills, conditioning, and repetition. The structure of this book follows that same logic.

Tennis Money 101 is organized like a long season, not a single match.

Each part builds on the one before it. Concepts are introduced in a deliberate order so you are not asked to make advanced decisions without first understanding the fundamentals. If you have ever trusted a training plan, this structure will feel familiar.

Front Matter: Setting the Mental Frame

The opening sections exist to reset expectations.

The foreword and introduction establish the mindset of the book. Money is not something you master all at once. It is something you manage point by point. These sections explain why financial decisions feel confusing after sports and why your athletic background is actually an advantage if you know how to use it.

Think of this as the pre-match warmup. You are not hitting winners yet. You are getting mentally ready.

Part I: Footwork and Fundamentals

Every great tennis player starts with the basics.

Part I focuses on foundational money skills. Understanding cash flow. Knowing where your money goes. Reducing unforced errors through budgeting and saving. Learning how credit, debt, and banking actually work.

This section is about control.

You cannot win rallies if your footwork is sloppy. You cannot build wealth if your fundamentals are unstable. Before investing or planning long term, you need clarity on your current position. These chapters are about awareness and consistency, not optimization.

If money has ever felt overwhelming, this is where things start to slow down.

Part II: Defense, Recovery, and Protection

Matches are often decided by who makes fewer mistakes.

Part II focuses on protection. Risk awareness. Insurance. Planning for setbacks. Understanding how to stay upright when things go wrong.

In tennis, defense is not passive. It is strategic. You recover. You reset. You stay in the point until the opportunity appears. Financially, protection plays the same role. Insurance, risk management, and smart decision making keep one mistake from turning into a loss.

This section helps you build resilience so that a single bad bounce does not derail your entire plan.

Part III: Constructing the Point (Investing Fundamentals)

Once fundamentals are solid, you start building offense.

Part III introduces investing. How markets actually work. The relationship between risk and return. Stocks, bonds, funds, real estate, and alternatives. These chapters emphasize efficiency over excitement.

In tennis, you do not win consistently by swinging for winners on every shot. You move the ball. You create openings. You trust patterns. Investing is framed the same way. This section teaches you how to think long term instead of chasing hot streaks or reacting emotionally.

You will not be asked to predict markets.

You will be taught how to behave within them.

Part IV: Managing the Match

Good players adjust without panic.

Part IV focuses on managing what you have built. Asset allocation. Buying and holding. Rebalancing. Handling momentum shifts. Managing emotions under pressure.

This is where many investors struggle, not because they lack knowledge, but because they lack discipline. These chapters emphasize systems, structure, and composure. Just like in a match, the goal is not to avoid losing points entirely, but to avoid spirals.

Execution matters most here.

Part V: The Long Season and Life Beyond the Court

Careers and finances do not exist in isolation.

Part V zooms out to the rest of life. Taxes. Retirement planning. Housing decisions. Career development. Family conversations. These chapters recognize that money decisions intersect with relationships, identity, and long term goals.

Tennis players understand seasons. Training blocks. Recovery periods. Career arcs. This section applies that thinking to life beyond competition and helps you plan for the future without fear.

Part VI: Winning the Match Over Time

The final section ties everything together.

Part VI focuses on long term success. When to seek help. How to recognize bad advice. Common mistakes that derail progress. Rules that consistently work.

This is not about one perfect match.

It is about building a sustainable approach that holds up over decades.

How to Use This Book

You can read this book straight through, or you can move section by section as needed. Like tennis training, repetition matters. You will see ideas reinforced across chapters because that is how habits form.

This playbook is not meant to sit on a shelf.

It is meant to be used.

Just like tennis, the results come from execution, not intention.

Point by point.

Decision by decision.

Season by season.

That is how the structure is designed, and that is how success is built.

About Pat Brown

Pat Brown's perspective on money was shaped long before he ever worked in financial services.

He played college football at the University of Kansas from 1994 to 1999 and was named team captain for the 1999 season. Life in the locker room taught him lessons that never left. Accountability was expected, not negotiated. Preparation mattered even when no one was watching. Discipline showed up in small decisions long before it showed up on Saturdays. Leadership was earned through consistency, not titles.

Those lessons translate cleanly to tennis.

Tennis teaches you that no one can win points for you. There is no hiding. Every decision, every adjustment, and every mistake belongs to you. That same reality exists in money once the structure of sports disappears.

After his playing career, Pat transitioned into financial services and built a career as a financial advisor and wealth manager. He works with individuals, families, business owners, and athletes who are navigating increasingly complex financial lives. His work includes financial planning, retirement income strategies, tax planning, insurance analysis, and philanthropic planning. Along the way, he pursued advanced education and professional development, earning an MBA and professional designations including ChFC®, RICP®, and CAP®.

What separates Pat's work from traditional financial education is not credentials. It is translation.

He understands what it feels like to leave a structured athletic environment and suddenly be responsible for every decision without a coach, a practice schedule, or a clear scoreboard. He understands delayed feedback, pressure, and the mental fatigue that comes from making hundreds of decisions without immediate results. He understands how disciplined athletes can still struggle financially, not because they lack work ethic, but because no one ever taught them how the financial game actually works.

That understanding became even more important as college sports changed.

With the introduction of Name, Image, and Likeness opportunities, student athletes began earning real income while still in school. Contracts, appearances, endorsement deals, and business entities arrived quickly. Financial education did not. Athletes were suddenly expected to manage taxes, cash flow, contracts, and long-term consequences without training or support.

Pat recognized the gap immediately.

That gap became the catalyst for his work in athlete financial education, particularly in the NIL space. He began focusing intentionally on teaching athletes and families how money actually works, using clear language and real-world scenarios instead of theory. His insights and work have been featured by national publications and platforms including Financial Planning, Yahoo, and ESPN Andscape, where he has shared perspectives on NIL planning, financial literacy gaps, and the challenges facing student athletes and their families.

From that work came a simple idea.

Athletes do not need more motivation.

They need a better playbook.

Athletes already understand preparation.

They already understand discipline.

They already understand long seasons, setbacks, adjustments, and pressure.

They just need financial education written in a language they already respect.

That belief led Pat to author a series of practical, athlete-focused books designed to meet athletes and families where they are. His NIL-related titles include Financial Literacy for NIL, Financial Literacy for NIL for Parents of Student Athletes, Financial Literacy for NIL for High School Students, and

Financial Literacy for NIL for International Student Athletes. Each book is intentionally clear, accessible, and grounded in real-life decisions athletes actually face.

In addition, Pat created a growing collection of sport-specific financial education titles. Each book translates the mindset, discipline, and culture of a specific sport into financial lessons that last beyond competition. Titles include Football Money 101, Baseball Money 101, Basketball Money 101, Cheer Money 101, Dance Money 101, Gymnastics Money 101, Hockey Money 101, Lacrosse Money 101, Rowing Money 101, Soccer Money 101, Softball Money 101, Tennis Money 101, Track Money 101, Volleyball Money 101, and Wrestling Money 101.

Each book follows the same philosophy.

You win with fundamentals.

You avoid unforced errors.

You manage momentum.

And you stay disciplined point after point.

To extend this mission beyond books, Pat founded Former Student Athlete, a platform created to support athletes navigating life after sports. Former Student Athlete focuses on education, community, and real-world resources related to financial literacy, career transitions, health, identity, and long-term success once the uniform comes off. The platform exists because leaving sports should not mean losing structure, support, or direction.

Pat regularly shares insights on athletes, money, and life after sports through public platforms including LinkedIn and Twitter and is easily found through a simple online search. For those interested in learning more, additional resources can be found at www.formerstudentathlete.com, www.financialliteracyfornil.com, and www.financialliteracyforstudentathletes.com.

At the center of Pat's work is a belief shaped by both sports and finance.

Athletes deserve a better playbook for life after competition.

And financial education should arrive before opportunity turns into regret.

That belief is the foundation of Tennis Money 101.

I

Part One

Part I: Footwork and Fundamentals

You cannot win matches without mastering the basics.

Every tennis player learns this lesson early, whether they listen or not.

You can have a big serve, flashy groundstrokes, and highlight-reel winners, but if your footwork is sloppy, the match eventually exposes you. Poor positioning leads to late contact. Late contact leads to unforced errors. Unforced errors turn close sets into losses.

Money works the same way.

Most financial problems are not caused by lack of effort or intelligence. They come from weak fundamentals. Athletes leave the sport with discipline, competitiveness, and a willingness to work, yet still struggle financially because the basics were never taught, reinforced, or practiced the way footwork was.

This first part of the book is about building that base.

In tennis, fundamentals are not glamorous. Split steps. Balance. Recovery steps. Court positioning. No one posts those clips online, but every high-level player obsesses over them. They know that when pressure hits, fundamentals are what hold everything together.

Financial fundamentals serve the same role.

Understanding where money comes from, where it goes, how it is stored, and how it moves is the equivalent of learning how to move efficiently on the court. You cannot play offense, defend consistently, or manage long matches if your base is unstable.

Most athletes were never given this training.

They were taught how to compete, how to train, how to push through fatigue, and how to respond to coaching. They were rarely taught how to manage cash flow, build saving habits, use credit responsibly, or understand banking systems. When money finally shows up, especially suddenly, it feels confusing and overwhelming, not because the athlete is careless, but because the instruction never happened.

That confusion creates bad habits.

In tennis, bad footwork causes you to reach instead of move. In money, weak fundamentals cause you to react instead of plan. You overspend, delay saving, misuse credit, or avoid decisions altogether. None of these feel catastrophic in the moment. Over time, they compound.

Part I is designed to slow everything down.

Before you invest.

Before you chase returns.

Before you worry about advanced strategies.

You learn how to stand correctly on the baseline.

This section focuses on understanding your financial snapshot, building basic systems, and reducing unforced errors. Budgeting is not about restriction. It is about court awareness. Banking is not about complexity. It is about knowing where the ball is at all times. Credit is not evil or magical. It is simply a tool that can either help or hurt depending on how it is used.

Discipline shows up here differently than in competition.

In tennis, discipline looks like drilling fundamentals even when you would rather play points. Financial discipline looks like automating savings, reviewing spending, and making boring decisions consistently. Neither feels exciting. Both win matches.

This part of the book emphasizes one central truth.

You do not win financially by swinging harder.

You win by making fewer mistakes.

Professional tennis players talk constantly about managing errors. They know that most matches are decided not by winners, but by who breaks down last. Money is the same. Financial success rarely comes from one big decision. It comes from avoiding repeated small mistakes over time.

Part I is where you learn to reduce those errors.

You will learn how to see the whole financial court, not just the ball in front of you. You will learn how to control possession through budgeting and saving. You will learn how credit and debt create pressure the same way poor positioning does in a rally. You will learn how banking systems support or undermine everything else you try to do.

This is not advanced strategy.

This is not theory.

This is repetition.

Just like footwork, these skills must be practiced, not admired. They form the base for every chapter that follows. Without them, investing becomes emotional, risk management becomes guesswork, and long-term planning becomes fragile.

With them, everything gets easier.

You move earlier.

You react less.

You stay balanced when the pace increases.

Before you can win points, games, or matches, you must control your movement. Before you can build wealth, you must control the basics. That is what this part is about.

Master the fundamentals.

Reduce unforced errors.

Stay balanced.

The rest of the match depends on it.

Chapter 1: Why Money Feels Confusing After Tennis

The first time it usually shows up is not dramatic.

It might be a paycheck that feels larger than anything you have managed before. It might be scholarship money, prize money, coaching income, NIL income, or a first real job after tennis. The number looks good. The confidence is there. And yet, underneath it, there is uncertainty.

You trained for tennis your entire life.

You did not train for money.

That disconnect is why money feels confusing for so many tennis players once the sport shifts, slows down, or ends.

The Opening Rally: Why This Feels Harder Than It Should

In tennis, confusion rarely comes from effort. It comes from unfamiliar situations. Different surfaces. Wind. A new opponent with an awkward style. The ball does not bounce the way you expect, and suddenly your timing is off.

Money feels the same way.

Athletes are taught how to work hard, compete, and respond to coaching. They are rarely taught how to read a pay stub, understand taxes, manage cash flow, or decide what to do with excess money. When those situations appear, there is no playbook and no coach on the sideline.

This is not a personal failure.

It is a training gap.

Financial literacy is often missing from athletic development because it is not part of the competitive pathway. Coaches are measured by wins. Programs are measured by results. Parents focus on performance, recruiting, and development. Money is treated as something to worry about later.

Later shows up fast.

Why Financial Literacy Is Rarely Taught to Athletes

Athletes live inside structured systems.

Practice times are set. Strength programs are prescribed. Travel schedules are handled. Meals are planned. In tennis academies and programs, much of life is organized around performance. That structure protects focus, but it also delays real-world decision-making.

Money decisions are often outsourced or ignored.

Parents handle accounts. Programs handle stipends. Scholarships reduce immediate pressure. When income arrives later, athletes are suddenly expected to perform in a new environment without reps.

In tennis terms, this is being asked to play a match without ever practicing on that surface.

You may still compete well.

You may still win points.

But the margin for error shrinks.

Money Myths Passed Through Clubs and Academies

When formal education is missing, myths fill the gap.

Tennis players hear the same financial myths repeated quietly through locker rooms, clubs, and academies.

"If you make enough, it will take care of itself."

"Saving is for people who are done competing."

"You have to take big risks to get ahead."

"Investing is basically gambling."

"I will deal with it once I have more money."

These myths sound reasonable in isolation. Over time, they create bad habits.

In tennis, bad habits develop when fundamentals are skipped. Players rely on timing or athleticism instead of footwork. It works until it does not. Money myths work the same way. They delay discipline and reward reaction.

Most financial mistakes are not reckless. They are inherited beliefs that were never challenged.

Saving vs Investing vs Gambling

One of the biggest sources of confusion is the difference between saving, investing, and gambling.

Saving is about safety and stability.

Investing is about long-term growth with a plan.

Gambling is about short-term outcomes driven by emotion.

In tennis terms, saving is recovery. It keeps you in the match. Investing is constructing points with intention. Gambling is going for low-percentage winners early in the rally.

Athletes are competitive by nature. That competitiveness can bleed into money decisions. Chasing hot stocks, crypto hype, or "can't miss" opportunities feels like swinging for winners. Sometimes it works. Often it does not.

The problem is not risk.

The problem is unplanned risk.

Professional tennis players do not avoid aggression. They choose when to attack. Financial success works the same way. Saving protects your position. Investing builds advantage. Gambling hands control to chance.

Confusion comes when those lines blur.

Why Consistency Beats Going for Winners Too Early

Every tennis player learns this lesson eventually.

Matches are not usually lost because someone did not hit enough winners. They are lost because someone made too many errors. The player who manages points, controls tempo, and stays disciplined usually wins over time.

Money follows the same pattern.

You do not build financial strength by making one brilliant decision. You build it by stacking small, boring, consistent actions over time. Saving regularly. Spending intentionally. Investing patiently. Avoiding emotional reactions.

Going for winners too early feels productive. It feels aggressive. It feels like progress. But without a base, it increases error rates.

Consistency does not look impressive on a highlight reel.

It looks impressive on a balance sheet.

This is especially hard for athletes because sports reward intensity. Money rewards endurance.

Coach's Perspective

A tennis coach would not sugarcoat this.

"Stop forcing shots."

"Build the point."

"Trust your legs."

"Make them miss."

"Play the long rally."

Financially, the advice is the same.

Do not force returns.

Do not chase what everyone else is chasing.

Do not skip the fundamentals.

Do not confuse activity with progress.

Discipline is not passive. It is intentional.

Game Situations and Decision Points

You get your first real paycheck or prize money. Do you spend first or plan first?

You hear about an investment opportunity everyone is talking about. Do you jump in or step back and evaluate?

You feel behind because others seem further along. Do you force a play or stick to your system?

Every one of these moments mirrors a tennis decision. Shot selection matters. Timing matters. Emotional control matters.

Common Athlete Mistakes and Financial Parallels

Tennis players force winners when impatient.

Financially, that shows up as chasing returns.

Players rely on talent instead of footwork.

Financially, that shows up as relying on income instead of systems.

Players avoid boring drills.

Financially, that shows up as avoiding budgeting and saving.

The pattern is the same. The environment changes. The habits follow.

Winning the Long Game

Money feels confusing after tennis because the scoring system changes.

There is no scoreboard.

There is no opponent across the net.

There is no coach calling timeouts.

But the skills that made you successful in tennis still apply.

Discipline.

Patience.

Preparation.

Consistency.

You do not need to win every point. You need to stay in the match long enough for discipline to work.

That is the mindset this book builds.

Athlete Takeaways

- Stop swinging for winners with your money. Build the point.
- Saving keeps you in the match. Investing builds advantage.
- Gambling is forcing shots without a plan.
- Consistency beats intensity over long matches.
- The fundamentals you avoided will decide the outcome.

Chapter 2: Read the Scoreline: Your Financial Snapshot

Every tennis player knows this moment.

You walk to the chair changeover and glance at the scoreboard. The score tells you more than just who is ahead. It tells you how the match has unfolded. Whether you are holding serve. Whether breaks are coming from mistakes or pressure. Whether momentum is real or fragile.

You cannot manage a match if you do not know the score.

Money works the same way. Before you improve anything, you have to read the scoreline of your financial life. Not what you think is happening. Not what you hope is happening. What is actually happening.

This chapter is about building your financial snapshot. It is not about judgment. It is about clarity.

Why Athletes Avoid the Financial Scoreboard

Many athletes avoid looking closely at their finances for the same reason players sometimes avoid the scoreboard during a rough stretch.

It creates discomfort.

If you are behind, you feel pressure.

If you are ahead, you worry about losing it.

If you are unsure, you hesitate.

Athletes are trained to respond to feedback in competition, but money feedback is quieter. There is no crowd reaction. No opponent across the net. Just numbers on a screen.

Ignoring the scoreboard does not change the score. It just removes your ability to adjust.

Income, Expenses, and Cash Flow

In tennis, momentum comes from controlling the flow of points. You manage tempo. You decide when to slow things down and when to apply pressure.

Cash flow works the same way.

Income is what comes in.

Expenses are what go out.

Cash flow is the difference between the two.

Positive cash flow gives you options. Negative cash flow creates pressure. Tight cash flow forces mistakes.

Athletes often focus on income first. How much am I making? How can I make more? Income matters, but it is only one side of the scoreboard.

Two players can earn the same income and end up in completely different positions depending on how they manage expenses.

In tennis terms, this is the difference between someone who wins points efficiently and someone who wins points but wastes energy. Both may get to the same game score. One is exhausted.

Understanding cash flow tells you whether you are winning points cleanly or grinding yourself into trouble.

Assets, Liabilities, and Net Worth

Net worth is the long-term score of your financial match.

Assets are what you own.

Liabilities are what you owe.

Net worth is the difference.

Assets include cash, investments, retirement accounts, and property. Liabilities include credit cards, loans, and any money you owe.

In tennis terms, assets are your strengths. Conditioning, footwork, shot variety, experience. Liabilities are your limitations. Injuries, technical flaws, mental leaks.

A strong net worth does not mean you are perfect. It means your strengths outweigh your weaknesses.

Athletes sometimes avoid net worth because it feels abstract. There is no daily feedback like a paycheck or a bill. But net worth is how progress compounds over time.

You can have strong income and weak net worth if spending and debt cancel it out. You can have modest income and strong net worth if discipline and consistency are in place.

The scoreboard you do not check still counts.

Fixed vs Variable Expenses

Every tennis match has constants and variables.

The court size does not change.

The rules do not change.

The opponent's style changes.

Expenses work the same way.

Fixed expenses are consistent. Rent, insurance, subscriptions, loan payments. They are predictable and recurring.

Variable expenses fluctuate. Food, travel, entertainment, gear, discretionary spending.

Problems arise when variable expenses behave like fixed ones. Lifestyle inflation locks in costs that reduce flexibility.

In tennis terms, this is committing to aggressive shot patterns regardless of score, surface, or opponent. It removes adaptability.

Athletes value flexibility on court. Financial flexibility comes from keeping fixed expenses manageable and variable expenses intentional.

Reviewing Where Your Money Actually Goes

This is the film study portion of money.

What you think you spend and what you actually spend are rarely the same.

Small expenses hide in plain sight. Subscriptions you forgot about. Convenience spending. Lifestyle creep that feels normal because it happened slowly.

Film never lies. Neither does transaction history.

Reviewing where your money goes is not about guilt. It is about awareness. Awareness creates control.

In tennis, players who watch film improve faster because they stop guessing. Financial clarity works the same way. Once you see patterns, decisions get easier.

You cannot fix what you refuse to see.

Coach's Perspective

A coach would be direct.

"Know the score."

"Stop guessing."

"Film doesn't lie."

"You can't adjust blind."

"Face it now or chase it later."

This is not about being perfect. It is about being honest.

Game Situations and Decision Points

You feel stressed about money but do not know why. Do you guess or review your cash flow?

You think you are doing fine because income is strong. Do you check net worth or assume progress?

You want more flexibility. Do you reduce fixed expenses or try to earn your way out?

Each of these moments mirrors in-match decisions. Awareness precedes adjustment.

Common Athlete Mistakes and Financial Parallels

Tennis players avoid the scoreboard when trailing.

Financially, that leads to avoidance.

Players blame conditions instead of reviewing film.

Financially, that leads to excuses.

Players focus on highlights instead of fundamentals.

Financially, that leads to income obsession instead of balance.

The pattern is the same. The discipline transfers.

Winning the Long Game

The financial snapshot is not a one-time exercise. It is a habit.

Strong players check the score regularly. They adjust between points, games, and sets. They do not wait until the match is over to realize what went wrong.

Money works the same way.

When you know your cash flow, understand your net worth, and see where money goes, you regain control. Control reduces stress. Reduced stress improves decision-making.

You do not need to be ahead to take control. You just need clarity.

Clarity is the start of every comeback.

Athlete Takeaways

- Read the financial scoreboard before changing your strategy.
- Cash flow controls momentum, not income alone.
- Net worth is the long-term match score.
- Fixed expenses limit flexibility if left unchecked.

- Film study applies to money too. Look at the data.

Chapter 3: Reducing Unforced Errors

Budgeting and Saving

Every tennis player knows the frustration of losing a match not because the opponent was better, but because of unforced errors. Balls into the net. Shots long by inches. Rushed decisions when patience would have won the point. The scoreboard does not care why the mistake happened. It just records the result.

Money mistakes work the same way.

Most financial problems are not caused by one catastrophic decision. They come from small, repeated errors. Inconsistent saving. Overspending without a plan. Letting habits slip because nothing bad happens immediately.

This chapter is about reducing unforced errors with money by building a budgeting and saving system that works even when motivation fades.

Budgeting Is Shot Selection, Not Restriction

Many athletes hear the word "budget" and immediately think restriction.

Less freedom.

Less fun.

More rules.

That reaction misses the point.

A budget is not about taking shots away. It is about choosing higher-percentage shots.

In tennis terms, budgeting is shot selection. You are not banned from hitting winners. You just stop going for low-percentage shots on every point.

Financially, a budget tells your money where to go before it disappears. It creates intention instead of reaction.

Without a budget, spending becomes emotional. You spend based on stress, boredom, reward, or convenience. That is how unforced errors pile up.

With a budget, decisions get easier. You already know what matters. You already know your limits.

The goal is not perfection. The goal is consistency.

Budgeting Systems That Actually Work

Just like tennis, there is no single perfect system. What works is the system you will actually use.

Some athletes prefer simple frameworks. Others like detail. The key is alignment with how your brain works.

A simple system might look like:

- Fixed expenses covered first
- Automatic saving second
- Everything else spent guilt-free within limits

A more detailed system might track categories monthly. Food. Travel. Training. Entertainment. Discretionary spending.

In tennis terms, this is choosing between aggressive baseline play or a more tactical, varied style. Both can win. What matters is discipline within the system.

The biggest mistake athletes make is building a budget they cannot maintain. Overly rigid systems break under pressure. Flexible systems survive long seasons.

If your budget collapses the first time life gets busy, it was never a good system.

Automating Savings Like Daily Drills

Great players do not rely on motivation to train fundamentals. They rely on routine.

Footwork drills.

Serve reps.

Conditioning work.

Saving works the same way.

Automation is the financial version of daily drills. Money moves to savings before you have time to think about it.

When saving is automatic, it stops competing with spending decisions. You do not have to choose discipline every month. The system chooses for you.

Athletes often wait until the end of the month to save what is left. That is like practicing after the match if you still have energy. It rarely happens.

Saving first is how you protect progress.

Even small automated amounts matter. Consistency beats intensity. A steady saving habit compounds quietly, just like reps over time.

Emergency Funds as Injury Protection

Every athlete understands injury risk.

You do not plan to get hurt, but you prepare for it. Proper warm-ups. Strength training. Recovery work.

An emergency fund is financial injury protection.

Unexpected expenses happen. Car repairs. Medical bills. Travel emergencies. Income disruptions. None of these mean you failed. They mean you live in the real world.

Without an emergency fund, every unexpected expense becomes a crisis. Credit cards get used. Debt grows. Stress spikes.

With an emergency fund, problems stay small.

In tennis terms, this is having physical durability. You may lose a point, but you stay in the match.

Emergency funds are not investments. They are not meant to grow aggressively. They exist to absorb shocks so your long-term plan stays intact.

Balancing Lifestyle With Long-Term Goals

One of the hardest skills for athletes is balancing enjoyment now with progress later.

You trained for years with delayed gratification. Then income shows up. Freedom increases. Spending feels like reward.

There is nothing wrong with enjoying money. The problem is when enjoyment crowds out the future.

In tennis terms, this is playing every point like match point in the first set. It feels exciting, but it is unsustainable.

A strong financial plan allows enjoyment without regret. That means:

- Spending intentionally
- Saving consistently
- Avoiding lifestyle commitments that limit flexibility

Balance does not mean equal spending and saving. It means aligning spending with values and goals.

If your lifestyle requires perfect income forever, it is fragile. Durable plans allow margin.

Coach's Perspective

A coach would simplify this quickly.

"Reduce unforced errors."

"Do the boring work."

"Reps matter."

"Discipline wins long matches."

"You don't need winners on every point."

Budgeting and saving are fundamentals. Nobody celebrates them. Everybody needs them.

Game Situations and Decision Points

You get a raise. Do you increase spending automatically or increase saving first?

You miss a savings goal one month. Do you quit the system or reset next point?

An unexpected expense hits. Do you use your emergency fund or reach for debt?

Each decision mirrors a point in a match. The choice you make determines momentum.

Common Athlete Mistakes and Financial Parallels

Tennis players go for winners too early.

Financially, that shows up as overspending.

Players abandon game plans after a few mistakes.

Financially, that shows up as quitting budgets.

Players rely on talent instead of discipline.

Financially, that shows up as income without structure.

The fix is the same. Return to fundamentals.

Winning the Long Game

Matches are not won by highlight shots alone. They are won by consistency, patience, and error reduction.

Money works the same way.

Budgeting gives structure. Saving builds resilience. Automation removes emotion. Emergency funds protect momentum.

You do not need to win every point. You need to avoid giving points away. Reducing unforced errors is how you stay in control of the match.

Athlete Takeaways

- Budgeting is shot selection, not restriction.
- Automation turns discipline into routine.
- Emergency funds keep small problems from becoming match-enders.
- Consistency beats intensity in saving.
- Long matches are won by reducing unforced errors.

Chapter 4: Credit, Debt, and Double Faults

Chapter 4: Credit, Debt, and Double Faults

How Small Mistakes Turn Into Lost Games

Every tennis player knows the feeling of a double fault at the worst possible moment.

You start the point in control. No rally yet. No pressure from the opponent. And then, two careless serves later, you hand over the point for free. No one hit a winner. No one earned it. You simply gave it away.

Debt works the same way.

Most financial losses are not caused by bold risks or unavoidable bad luck. They are caused by avoidable mistakes with credit and debt. Missed payments. High-interest balances. Poor understanding of how credit actually works. These mistakes quietly add up until momentum is gone and the match slips away.

This chapter is about understanding credit and debt so you stop giving points away.

Credit Scores and Reports: The Scoreboard You Cannot Ignore

In tennis, you always know the score. Love–15. 30–all. Break point. The scoreboard shapes decisions whether you like it or not.

In the financial world, your credit score plays that same role.

A credit score is not a judgment of your character. It is a record of your behavior. It reflects how consistently you borrow and repay money over time.

Your credit report shows:

- Whether you pay on time
- How much you owe
- How long you have used credit
- How often you apply for new credit

Your score rises with consistency and falls with mistakes.

Many athletes ignore credit because it feels abstract. You cannot see it. No one talks about it in locker rooms. Until suddenly it matters. Renting an apartment. Buying a car. Applying for a mortgage. Even some jobs.

In tennis terms, this is ignoring the score until you realize you are down a break.

You do not have to obsess over your credit score, but you cannot ignore it. It is part of the game whether you want it to be or not.

Credit Cards, Loans, and Interest: How the Rally Actually Works

Credit itself is not the enemy. Misunderstanding it is.

Credit cards and loans allow you to borrow money now and repay it later. The cost of that convenience is interest.

Interest is the price you pay for using someone else's money.

Here is where athletes get tripped up.

Minimum payments feel manageable. Monthly payments look small. The total cost gets hidden.

In tennis terms, this is playing short points without realizing how many games are still left in the set.

High-interest debt, especially credit cards, compounds against you. The longer you carry balances, the more expensive they become. Payments go mostly toward interest early on. Progress feels slow even when you are "doing the right thing."

Loans like auto loans or student loans can be more structured, but they still require discipline. Missed payments damage credit. Long terms increase total cost.

Understanding interest changes behavior. When you see debt as an opponent that gets stronger over time, you stop treating it casually.

Good Debt vs Bad Debt: Not All Borrowing Is the Same

Athletes often hear phrases like "all debt is bad" or "leverage is smart." Both are oversimplifications.

The difference between good debt and bad debt comes down to purpose, cost, and impact on flexibility.

Good debt typically:

- Has lower interest rates
- Supports long-term goals
- Does not crush cash flow
- Has a clear payoff plan

Bad debt typically:

- Has high interest rates
- Funds short-term consumption
- Reduces flexibility
- Lingers without a plan

In tennis terms, good debt is like playing a high-percentage rally to set up a better position later. Bad debt is going for low-percentage shots under pressure and hoping it works out.

A student loan that supports a degree leading to stable income can be useful. Credit card debt from lifestyle spending rarely is.

The key is intention. Borrowing without a plan turns even "good" debt into a problem.

Debt Mistakes That Cost Games

Most debt problems come from predictable mistakes.

One is using credit to maintain a lifestyle your income cannot support. This creates pressure that never fully goes away.

Another is focusing only on monthly payments instead of total cost. Longer terms feel easier but quietly cost more.

Another is ignoring small balances. A few thousand dollars at high interest can do more damage than a large, structured loan.

And perhaps the most common mistake is pretending debt will fix itself.

In tennis terms, this is hoping the opponent misses instead of playing disciplined points.

Debt does not disappear on its own. It requires a plan.

Creating a Debt Strategy That Restores Control

Just like tennis, the goal is not to avoid every challenge. It is to manage them intelligently.

A strong debt strategy starts with clarity:

- What do you owe?
- At what interest rates?
- What are the minimums?
- What can you realistically pay extra?

From there, you choose a system.

Some athletes prefer attacking highest-interest debt first to stop the bleeding. Others prefer eliminating small balances first to build momentum.

Both approaches work if you stay consistent.

The mistake is bouncing between strategies without commitment. That creates frustration and delay.

Consistency restores control. Control restores confidence.

Coach's Perspective

A coach would be blunt.

"Stop giving points away."

"Know the score."

"Protect your serve."

"Discipline beats panic."

"You don't win matches with double faults."

Credit and debt are not emotional topics. They are execution topics.

Game Situations and Decision Points

You are offered a credit card increase. Do you see opportunity or added risk?

You want something now. Do you borrow without a plan or wait and save?

You miss a payment deadline. Do you ignore it or correct immediately?

Each decision mirrors a pressure point in a match. Small choices swing momentum.

Common Athlete Mistakes and Financial Parallels

Tennis players rush serves under pressure.

Financially, that shows up as impulsive borrowing.

Players focus on power instead of placement.

Financially, that shows up as high-interest debt.

Players avoid fixing weaknesses.

Financially, that shows up as ignoring balances.

The solution is the same. Slow down. Reset. Execute fundamentals.

Winning the Long Game

You do not need perfect credit. You need consistent behavior.

You do not need zero debt immediately. You need a plan that reduces risk over time.

Matches are lost through double faults, not tough rallies. Financial stability works the same way.

When you understand credit, manage debt intentionally, and avoid repeated mistakes, you stop handing points away.

That is how you stay competitive over the long season.

Athlete Takeaways

- Credit scores are the scoreboard whether you like it or not.
- Interest compounds against you when you lose discipline.
- Not all debt is equal, but all debt needs a plan.
- Double faults with money cost games quietly.
- Control credit, reduce mistakes, and protect momentum.

Chapter 5: The Equipment Bag of Money

Banking Basics That Keep You Match-Ready

Every tennis player knows the importance of their equipment bag. You do not just throw racquets, shoes, grips, and water bottles into a random pile and hope it works out. Everything has a place. You know what is used for warm-ups, what is saved for match play, and what stays in the bag for emergencies. When something is missing or disorganized, it shows up at the worst possible time.

Your bank accounts work the same way.

Checking, savings, transfers, and protections are not exciting topics, but they are foundational. Poor banking setup leads to missed payments, overdrafts, stress, and mistakes that distract you from everything else. A clean system keeps your financial game simple and efficient.

This chapter is about understanding your banking equipment so nothing breaks down mid-match.

Checking vs Savings Accounts: Knowing Which Tool to Use

A checking account is your daily-use racquet.

Money flows in. Money flows out. Bills, rent, groceries, subscriptions, and transfers all run through checking. It is designed for movement, not long-term storage.

A savings account is your backup gear.

It is not meant to be touched constantly. It exists to hold money for future use, emergencies, or short-term goals. The separation matters. When savings sits too close to spending, it disappears faster.

In tennis terms, checking is the rally racquet. Savings is the one you protect for big points.

Common mistakes happen when athletes blur these roles. Keeping everything in one account makes it hard to track progress and easy to overspend. Constantly dipping into savings feels harmless until it becomes habit.

The fix is simple. Use checking for transactions. Use savings for protection and planning.

Clarity reduces unforced errors.

Online Banks vs Traditional Banks: Choosing the Right Court

Not all banks operate the same way.

Traditional banks offer physical branches, tellers, and in-person service. Online banks focus on digital access, lower overhead, and often higher interest rates on savings.

Neither is automatically better.

Traditional banks can be useful if you:

- Need cash deposits regularly
- Prefer face-to-face support
- Value branch access

Online banks can be useful if you:

- Manage money digitally
- Want higher savings yields
- Prefer fewer fees

In tennis terms, this is choosing between different court surfaces. Hard court, clay, or grass. Each changes how the game plays, but the fundamentals stay the same.

The mistake is staying with a bank out of habit instead of fit. Fees, low interest, and poor service quietly drain momentum.

You are allowed to choose the environment that supports your style of play.

How Money Moves Electronically: The Hidden Rally

Most money movement today is invisible.

Direct deposit. Automatic bill pay. Transfers between accounts. Peer-to-peer apps. Credit card payments. These are the rallies you do not see but rely on every day.

When set up correctly, electronic movement creates consistency. When ignored, it creates confusion.

Automatic deposits ensure money shows up on time. Automatic payments prevent missed bills. Transfers move savings without relying on willpower.

In tennis terms, this is footwork.

You rarely think about it when it works. You feel it immediately when it does not.

Many athletes avoid automation because they want control. Ironically, automation often creates more control by reducing mistakes.

The key is review, not micromanagement. You set systems, check them periodically, and adjust when needed.

That is professional behavior.

Overdrafts: Losing Points You Never Played

An overdraft happens when more money leaves your account than you have available.

It feels small. It happens fast. And it is expensive.

Overdraft fees are penalties for poor timing. They do not mean you are irresponsible. They mean the system failed.

In tennis terms, this is double-faulting a game away because you were not watching the score.

The fix is structural, not emotional.

Simple protections include:

- Keeping a buffer in checking
- Linking savings as backup
- Turning off optional overdraft coverage

You do not want your bank profiting from your mistakes. Clean structure prevents unnecessary penalties.

Fraud Protection: Guarding Against the Unexpected

Fraud is not about intelligence. It is about exposure.

Card skimmers. Data breaches. Phishing emails. Stolen information. These events happen to disciplined people all the time.

Banks offer protections for a reason.

Alerts for transactions. Spending notifications. Account monitoring. Quick freeze options. These tools exist to catch problems early.

In tennis terms, this is injury prevention.

You do not train expecting to get hurt, but you prepare for it anyway.

Ignoring fraud protection does not make you safer. Awareness and quick response do.

Building a Simple, Match-Ready Banking System

A strong banking setup is boring by design.

It usually includes:

- One primary checking account for bills and spending
- One savings account for emergencies
- Optional secondary savings for short-term goals

- Automatic deposits and payments
- Regular review

This structure reduces decisions, stress, and mistakes.

Athletes often overcomplicate money early, chasing optimization before fundamentals. That leads to confusion and dropped points.

Simple systems win long matches.

Coach's Perspective

A coach would not overthink this.

"Know your equipment."

"Don't change racquets every game."

"Protect your gear."

"Details matter."

"Stop beating yourself."

Banking basics are execution, not creativity.

Game Situations and Decision Points

You see a fee on your account. Do you ignore it or fix the structure?

You keep overdrafting. Do you blame discipline or adjust systems?

You get a fraud alert. Do you act immediately or assume it is nothing?

These are momentum moments. How you respond matters.

Common Athlete Mistakes and Financial Parallels

Players ignore their gear until it fails.

Financially, that shows up as poor banking setup.

Players resist routine.

Financially, that shows up as missed payments.

Players chase complexity.

Financially, that shows up as unnecessary accounts and apps.

Fundamentals always matter.

Winning the Long Game

Banking is not where you win matches, but it is where you lose them if ignored.

Clean systems reduce distractions. Protected accounts prevent setbacks. Automation builds consistency.

When your equipment bag is organized, you can focus on the match.

That is the goal.

Athlete Takeaways

- Checking is for movement, savings is for protection.
- Choose banks that fit your game, not your habits.
- Automation reduces unforced errors.
- Overdrafts and fraud are system problems, not effort problems.
- Clean banking keeps you match-ready over a long season.

Part II: Defense, Recovery, and Protection

Matches Are Often Won by Who Makes Fewer Mistakes

At higher levels of tennis, matches are rarely decided by highlight-reel winners.

They are decided by consistency. By who recovers better between points. By who manages their body, energy, and errors over long rallies and long matches. The player who stays healthy, composed, and protected usually outlasts the one swinging freely with no margin.

Money works the same way.

Most financial outcomes are not destroyed by one catastrophic decision. They erode through preventable mistakes. Gaps in protection. Ignored risks. Events that could have been managed but were not. Defense is not flashy, but it is decisive.

This section is about protecting what you are building so one bad bounce does not end the match.

Why Defense Matters More Than You Think

Every tennis player trains offense.

Serve speed. Forehands. Winners. Aggression. But the longer you play, the more you realize how important defense really is. Good footwork. Recovery speed. Shot tolerance. The ability to stay in the point even when you are stretched.

Financially, defense is everything that prevents setbacks from becoming disasters.

Medical bills. Accidents. Lawsuits. Loss of income. Unexpected repairs. These are not hypothetical risks. They are normal life events. The question is not if something happens. It is how prepared you are when it does.

In tennis terms, defense keeps you alive in points you should not win. Financial defense keeps you intact during seasons you did not plan for.

Recovery Between Points and Recovery Between Financial Hits

Tennis is a game of constant recovery.

You sprint, you hit, you recover. You do not panic after losing a point. You reset. Bounce the ball. Control your breathing. Prepare for the next rally.

Financial recovery works the same way.

Without protection, one unexpected expense can derail progress for months or years. With protection, setbacks become manageable interruptions instead of season-ending injuries.

Insurance, emergency savings, and risk planning are recovery tools. They allow you to stay in the match even after taking a hit.

Athletes who ignore recovery burn out. People who ignore financial protection get stuck playing defense forever.

Protection Is About Margin, Not Fear

Many athletes resist protection because it feels pessimistic.

They would rather focus on upside. Growth. Opportunity. But defense is not fear-based. It is margin-based. It gives you room to make aggressive plays without risking collapse.

In tennis terms, this is playing with net clearance.

You still attack. You still go for your shots. But you give yourself enough margin that one miss does not spiral into a breakdown.

Financial protection creates that margin.

When you know you can handle a medical bill, a repair, or a temporary loss of income, you make better decisions everywhere else. Pressure drops. Confidence improves. Execution sharpens.

Common Financial Mistakes Come From Ignoring Defense

Most financial stress comes from gaps, not complexity.

No health coverage.

No emergency fund.

No disability protection.

No liability coverage.

No plan for income interruption.

These gaps force people into bad decisions. High-interest debt. Early withdrawals. Selling investments at the wrong time. Taking jobs they hate out of necessity.

In tennis terms, this is playing a long match without hydration, nutrition, or recovery. Eventually, something gives.

Defense allows offense to work.

Why Athletes Are Especially Vulnerable Here

Athletes are trained to push through discomfort.

Play hurt.

Ignore fatigue.

Compete anyway.

That mindset builds toughness, but it can backfire financially. Many athletes assume they will "figure it out" if something happens. That assumption is costly.

Money does not respond to grit the way competition does.

Bills do not care how tough you are. Recovery requires preparation, not toughness.

The strongest competitors build protection early so they can keep competing later.

Defense Is Invisible Until You Need It

No one celebrates defense until it saves the match.

A deep rally ball.

A sliding retrieval.

A forced error.

Financial protection works the same way. You rarely feel its value day to day. You feel it immediately when something goes wrong and you are still standing.

That is the point.

Good defense keeps the match boring in the best way.

Coach's Perspective

A coach would frame it clearly.

"Stay in the point."

"Make them hit one more ball."

"Recover between points."

"Don't beat yourself."

"Defense wins matches."

Protection is not optional at higher levels. It is expected.

Game Situations and Decision Points

You get injured. Do you have coverage or chaos?

Your income pauses. Do you have recovery time or panic?

An accident happens. Are you protected or exposed?

Defense determines how long you can stay in the match.

Winning the Long Game

Offense gets attention. Defense wins seasons.

Financial protection does not make you rich. It keeps you from getting knocked out. It preserves momentum. It gives you space to play your game without fear.

This section is about building that foundation.

Make fewer mistakes.

Recover faster.

Stay in the match.

That is how long matches are won.

Chapter 6: Risk Awareness and Shot Selection

Every tennis player learns this lesson the hard way.

You step inside the baseline, see an opening, and go for too much. The shot feels right in the moment. The swing is aggressive. The intent is confident. And then the ball sails long. Unforced error.

Great players are not the ones who never attack. They are the ones who understand **when** to attack and **when** to rally. They read the situation. They respect the scoreline. They choose shots that fit the moment, not just their ego.

Money works the same way.

Most financial mistakes are not about ignorance. They are about poor shot selection. Taking risk at the wrong time. Playing too defensively when growth is needed. Letting emotion dictate decisions instead of context.

Risk awareness is learning how to choose the right financial shot at the right time.

Emotional Risk vs Financial Risk

In tennis, emotional risk and technical risk are not the same thing.

Emotional risk is how a shot *feels*.

Financial risk is how a decision *actually behaves* over time.

A forehand down the line might feel dangerous because you missed one earlier. A defensive slice might feel safe even though it puts you on your heels. Feelings lie. Film does not.

Financially, emotional risk shows up as fear, excitement, or overconfidence. Financial risk is the real probability of loss, volatility, and long-term impact.

Many athletes avoid investing because it *feels* risky. Others chase hot opportunities because they *feel* confident. Both confuse emotion with reality.

In tennis terms, this is letting nerves choose your shots instead of the score, opponent, and court position.

Risk awareness means separating how something feels from how it actually performs.

Time Horizon Is Your Court Position

Where you are on the court matters.

When you are inside the baseline with time, you can attack. When you are stretched wide or pushed deep, you rally and reset.

Time horizon works the same way financially.

If you need money soon, risk matters more. If your timeline is long, volatility matters less. The mistake is playing short-term shots with long-term money or long-term shots with short-term needs.

Young athletes often have the equivalent of a deep court position and plenty of time. They can absorb volatility. Older athletes or those with near-term goals need better positioning and margin.

In tennis terms, time horizon is court awareness. You do not hit the same shot from every position.

Flexibility Is Recovery Speed

Good defenders recover quickly.

They might be out of position for a moment, but they get back into balance before the next shot. Poor defenders get stuck scrambling.

Financial flexibility is your recovery speed.

Cash reserves. Stable income. Low fixed expenses. These things give you time to react instead of forcing bad shots.

When flexibility is low, every decision feels urgent. When flexibility is high, you can choose smarter shots.

Many risky financial decisions come from lack of flexibility, not lack of intelligence.

In tennis terms, this is playing tired and late to every ball. Eventually, you force something you should not.

How Risk Touches Every Money Decision

Risk is not just about investing.

It shows up in:

- Taking on debt
- Choosing a job
- Buying a home
- Starting a business
- Delaying savings
- Ignoring insurance

Every decision has a risk profile. The question is whether you are aware of it.

Athletes are trained to evaluate risk constantly. You decide when to go big, when to play safe, and when to reset. Money deserves the same awareness.

Ignoring risk does not eliminate it. It just makes outcomes unpredictable.

Knowing When to Attack

There are moments when attacking makes sense.

You have time.

You have margin.

You understand the downside.

You can recover if it does not work.

Financial attacks might include:

- Investing aggressively early in your career
- Taking a calculated career risk
- Starting a business with a safety net
- Increasing savings after a raise

These are not reckless moves. They are intentional plays made from a strong position.

In tennis terms, this is stepping inside the baseline on a short ball.

Knowing When to Rally

Rallying is not passive.

It is strategic. It keeps you alive in the point. It wears down the opponent. It sets up better opportunities later.

Financial rallying includes:

- Staying invested during volatility
- Focusing on saving instead of chasing returns
- Paying down debt
- Building emergency reserves
- Simplifying decisions

Many athletes struggle here because rallying feels boring. But long matches are won in rallies, not highlight shots.

Risk Does Not Mean Avoidance

Playing safe does not mean playing scared.

Great players are aggressive **within structure**. They take risks that fit the situation and avoid risks that create unnecessary errors.

Financial discipline is the same.

Risk awareness is not about eliminating risk. It is about **choosing** risk intentionally.

Coach's Perspective

A coach would say it clearly.

"Pick better shots."

"Know the score."

"Play the court."

"Don't force it."

"Make them earn it."

"High percentage wins."

Risk awareness is maturity.

Game Situations and Decision Points

Markets drop. Do you panic or rally?

You get a raise. Do you spend it or reposition?

You see someone else winning big. Do you chase or stick to your plan?

Every moment asks the same question. What shot fits this situation?

Common Athlete Mistakes and Financial Parallels

Athletes force winners.

Financially, that means chasing returns.

Athletes play scared after mistakes.

Financially, that means avoiding growth forever.

Athletes ignore positioning.

Financially, that means ignoring time horizon and flexibility.

Errors compound when awareness disappears.

Winning the Long Game

Tennis matches are won by players who manage risk better than their opponents.

They stay composed. They pick their spots. They rally when needed and attack when it counts.

Financial success works the same way.

You do not need perfect shots. You need smart ones.

Athlete Takeaways

- Shot selection matters more than raw power
- Risk feels emotional but behaves mathematically
- Time horizon is court positioning
- Flexibility improves recovery and decision-making
- Rallying wins more matches than forcing winners

Chapter 7: Insurance Fundamentals Every Player Needs

Every tennis player understands protection, even if they do not call it that.

You tape your ankles before long matches. You manage workloads to avoid injury. You warm up properly, cool down intentionally, and listen to small warning signs before they turn into something bigger. None of that guarantees you will never get hurt. It simply reduces the damage when something unexpected happens.

Insurance works the same way.

Insurance is not about pessimism. It is about protecting your ability to keep playing the match when something goes wrong. Most financial plans do not fail because of bad investing. They fail because of one uncovered event that knocks everything off course.

This chapter is about understanding insurance as defensive tennis. It is not flashy. It does not win points outright. But without it, one bad moment can end the match.

Health Insurance: Your Baseline Protection

Health insurance is the foundation.

In tennis terms, this is your baseline positioning. Without it, every rally becomes dangerous. A simple injury or illness can turn into a financial disaster.

Health insurance helps cover doctor visits, hospital stays, prescriptions, and preventative care. Plans differ, but they generally include premiums, deductibles, copays, and out-of-pocket maximums.

Many athletes make the mistake of choosing plans based only on monthly cost. That is like choosing shoes based only on looks. Comfort, durability, and fit matter more over time.

If you train hard, compete, or simply live an active life, you will use healthcare. Health insurance is not optional defense. It is table stakes.

Auto and Renters Insurance: Protecting the Environment Around You

Auto insurance exists because mistakes happen.

You can be a great driver and still get hit by someone else. You can follow the rules and still be part of an accident. Auto insurance protects you from financial liability and helps cover damage and injuries.

In tennis terms, this is protecting the court around you. You might not cause the problem, but you are still in the match when it happens.

Renters insurance is often overlooked, especially by younger athletes. It protects your belongings and provides liability coverage if someone gets hurt in your space.

Many people skip renters insurance because it feels unnecessary. That is like skipping stretching because you feel fine today. The cost is small. The protection is meaningful.

Homeowners Insurance: Playing a Longer Match

Homeownership introduces new responsibilities.

Homeowners insurance protects the structure, your belongings, and your liability. It also covers certain natural disasters and accidents, depending on the policy.

In tennis terms, owning a home is playing a longer match with more variables. Weather, maintenance, and wear all come into play.

Underinsuring a home is common. So is misunderstanding what is actually covered. Insurance should be reviewed when major life changes happen, not ignored once purchased.

Deductibles, Premiums, and Coverage Limits Explained

Understanding how insurance works matters.

Premiums are what you pay to stay in the match. Deductibles are what you pay before coverage kicks in. Coverage limits define how much protection you actually have.

Choosing insurance is about tradeoffs.

Lower premiums often mean higher deductibles. Higher coverage limits usually cost more. The right balance depends on your financial flexibility.

In tennis terms, this is choosing your equipment setup. String tension, racket weight, and grip size all affect performance. There is no universal best choice. There is only what fits your game.

If a deductible would force you into debt or drain savings, it is too high. If coverage limits would not protect you in a worst-case scenario, they are too low.

Insurance Is Risk Transfer, Not Risk Elimination

Insurance does not remove risk.

It transfers risk from you to an insurance company. That transfer allows you to keep playing the long match even if you lose a point badly.

Many athletes misunderstand this. They either expect insurance to cover everything or assume it is useless because it does not.

In tennis terms, insurance is not a guarantee you win the point. It is a guarantee you get to play the next one.

Common Insurance Gaps Athletes Face

Athletes and former athletes often miss coverage in predictable ways.

They rely on parents' plans without knowing when coverage ends. They skip renters insurance. They choose the cheapest option without understanding tradeoffs. They fail to update policies after life changes.

These gaps show up under pressure.

Insurance should be boring. If it becomes exciting, something went wrong.

Insurance as Defensive Discipline

Defense wins matches.

Not every point is about aggression. Sometimes the smartest play is staying in the rally and forcing the opponent to make a mistake.

Insurance is defensive discipline for your financial life. It protects progress you have already made and prevents one event from undoing years of work.

Coach's Perspective

A coach would not sugarcoat it.

"Protect yourself."

"Availability matters."

"You can't win if you're injured."

"Handle your business."

"Defense is effort."

Skipping insurance is not confidence. It is exposure.

Game Situations and Decision Points

You feel healthy. Do you carry coverage anyway?

You want lower monthly costs. Do you understand the deductible risk?

Your life changes. Do you update coverage or assume it is fine?

Defense matters most when you least expect it.

Common Athlete Mistakes and Financial Parallels

Athletes skip recovery work.

Financially, that means skipping insurance.

Athletes underestimate wear and tear.

Financially, that means underinsuring.

Athletes play through pain until it becomes injury.

Financially, that means ignoring coverage gaps until crisis.

Winning the Long Game

Insurance does not make you wealthy.

It keeps you from losing everything.

That alone makes it one of the most important fundamentals in your financial plan. You cannot build offense without defense. You cannot plan long-term without protection.

The best players rarely talk about defense. They just have it.

Athlete Takeaways

- Insurance is defense, not negativity
- Health coverage is baseline positioning
- Deductibles and limits define real protection
- Small premiums prevent big setbacks
- You cannot win the long match without staying protected

Chapter 8: Life, Disability, and Liability Protection

Every tennis player understands that the match can change in an instant.

One awkward slide. One mistimed landing. One strain that does not heal the way it should. You can be playing the best tennis of your life and still find yourself sidelined by something you never saw coming. That reality is not fear based. It is experience based.

Life, disability, and liability insurance exist for the same reason you train smart and recover properly. They protect what you have built and preserve your ability to keep competing, even when circumstances change.

This chapter is about protecting income, protecting people who depend on you, and protecting yourself from risks that can quietly derail everything else.

Term vs Permanent Life Insurance: Understanding the Purpose

Life insurance is not about you. It is about everyone else.

If people depend on your income, your presence, or your financial support, life insurance becomes a responsibility. It replaces income, pays off debts, and creates stability during chaos.

There are two primary types of life insurance.

Term life insurance provides coverage for a specific period of time. It is straightforward. You pay a premium, and if something happens during the term, the benefit pays out. It is usually affordable and effective for protecting income during working years.

Permanent life insurance lasts for life and includes additional features like cash value. It is more complex and more expensive. It can play a role in certain planning situations, but it is not automatically better.

In tennis terms, term insurance is your reliable rally ball. Simple. Effective. Gets the job done. Permanent insurance is a specialty shot. Useful in the right hands and situations, but unnecessary for most players early on.

The biggest mistake athletes make is buying life insurance without understanding why. Insurance should solve a specific problem, not exist because someone sold it convincingly.

Disability Insurance: Protecting Your Most Valuable Asset

Your ability to earn income is your greatest financial asset.

Not your savings. Not your investments. Your income.

Disability insurance protects that asset. It replaces a portion of your income if you are unable to work due to injury or illness.

Most athletes underestimate this risk. They assume disability means something catastrophic. In reality, many disabilities come from common issues. Back problems. Joint injuries. Chronic conditions. Mental health challenges.

In tennis terms, this is protecting your dominant hand. You can have the best strategy in the world, but if you cannot swing the racket, the match is over.

Employer provided disability coverage is often limited. Individual coverage can fill gaps, especially for high earners or those with specialized careers.

If your income stopped tomorrow, how long could you maintain your lifestyle? Disability insurance answers that question before you have to live it.

Umbrella Liability Coverage: Extra Defense When Things Escalate

Liability risk increases as life gets bigger.

More assets. More income. More visibility. More responsibility.

Umbrella insurance provides additional liability coverage beyond auto and homeowners policies. It protects you if a lawsuit exceeds standard limits.

Many athletes assume this only matters for wealthy people. That is a mistake. Lawsuits do not target net worth. They target opportunity.

In tennis terms, umbrella coverage is playing with extra margin over the net. You are not changing your game. You are reducing the chance one mistake costs you the match.

Umbrella policies are often inexpensive relative to the protection they provide. They exist for low probability, high impact events. That is exactly when insurance matters most.

How These Coverages Work Together

Insurance is not about individual policies. It is about coordination.

Life insurance protects people who depend on you. Disability insurance protects income while you are alive. Liability insurance protects assets you are building.

In tennis terms, this is court coverage. Singles players still move side to side. Doubles players still communicate and cover space. No area is ignored.

A gap in coverage is like leaving half the court open and hoping the opponent does not notice.

Common Insurance Mistakes Athletes Make

The mistakes are predictable.

Waiting too long. Buying too much of the wrong thing. Skipping coverage because it feels unnecessary. Relying on employer benefits without understanding limitations. Never reviewing policies after life changes.

Athletes are used to feeling invincible. Insurance planning forces humility.

That discomfort causes delay.

In tennis terms, this is refusing to practice defense because offense feels more fun. Eventually, the weakness gets exposed.

Insurance Is About Control, Not Fear

Good insurance planning creates freedom.

It allows you to take career risks. Invest long term. Sleep better. Focus on improvement instead of fear.

Insurance is not an admission that something bad will happen. It is an acknowledgment that if it does, you are prepared.

In tennis terms, confidence comes from preparation. Not denial.

Coach's Perspective

A coach would be direct.

"Protect your ability to compete."

"Handle your business off the court."

"Availability matters."

"Control what you can control."

"Do not beat yourself."

Ignoring insurance is not toughness. It is exposure.

Game Situations and Decision Points

You have dependents. Do you protect them or assume nothing will change?

You earn a strong income. Do you insure it or hope health holds forever?

Your assets grow. Do you increase protection or rely on minimum coverage?

These decisions rarely feel urgent until they are unavoidable.

Common Athlete Mistakes and Financial Parallels

Athletes play through injury.

Financially, that means ignoring disability risk.

Athletes underestimate opponents.

Financially, that means underestimating liability exposure.

Athletes chase flash over fundamentals.

Financially, that means buying complex insurance without purpose.

Winning the Long Game

You do not win long matches by taking unnecessary risks.

You win by staying available, protecting your strengths, and managing downside so you can keep playing aggressively when it counts.

Life, disability, and liability insurance do not make headlines. They preserve progress. They protect momentum. They keep one bad moment from becoming a permanent loss.

That is winning defense.

Athlete Takeaways

- Income is your dominant hand, protect it
- Life insurance is about others, not you
- Disability coverage protects your ability to stay in the match
- Umbrella insurance adds margin when stakes rise
- Smart defense keeps you playing long after setbacks

Part III: Constructing the Point (Investing Fundamentals)

High-percentage shots win more points than flashy winners.

Every tennis player learns this lesson the hard way.

You can hit spectacular winners in warmups. You can light up practice courts with pace and spin. But when the match starts, especially against a disciplined opponent, the player who wins is rarely the one going for highlight shots on every ball. It is the player who constructs points. The one who moves the opponent, manages risk, waits for the right opening, and understands that winning tennis is about percentages, not perfection.

Investing works the same way.

This part of the book is not about quick money, hot streaks, or guessing the next breakout opportunity. It is about understanding how the investing "point" is built and why patience, positioning, and discipline matter more than raw aggression.

Why Investing Is a Long Rally, Not a Single Shot

Many athletes approach investing the way beginners approach tennis.

They look for winners.

They chase speed.

They assume aggression equals success.

In tennis, that mindset leads to unforced errors. In investing, it leads to losses, stress, and inconsistent results.

Markets reward investors who can stay in rallies. That means accepting volatility, managing risk, and letting probabilities work over time. Just like tennis, most points are not decided by winners. They are decided by mistakes.

High-percentage investing focuses on avoiding the big errors that end the match early.

Stocks, Bonds, and Ownership as Shot Selection

In tennis, you choose shots based on situation.

A forehand inside the baseline is different than a running backhand on the stretch. The score matters. Your opponent matters. Your conditioning matters.

Financially, stocks, bonds, and other investments are simply different shot selections.

Stocks are aggressive shots. They drive growth, but they come with volatility.

Bonds are rally balls. They stabilize performance and reduce swings.

Diversified funds are consistency plays. They reduce reliance on any one outcome.

None of these are "good" or "bad." They are situational. Problems arise when investors expect every shot to be a winner or panic when rallies get long.

Market Cycles Are Momentum Shifts, Not Match Enders

Every tennis match has momentum swings.

You can play a great game and still lose it. You can struggle early and still win the set. What matters is how you respond to momentum changes.

Market cycles work the same way.

There are periods of growth, periods of stagnation, and periods of decline. These are not signs that the system is broken. They are part of how markets function.

Investors who treat every downturn like match point against them tend to abandon their strategy at the worst time. Those who understand cycles stay composed, adjust when needed, and keep playing the point.

Long-Term Strategy vs Chasing Hot Streaks

Every tennis player has faced an opponent on a heater.

Shots are landing. Confidence is high. The temptation is to change everything. Swing harder. Go for more. Force plays.

That usually makes things worse.

In investing, hot stocks, trending strategies, and market hype create the same temptation. Chasing what just worked often means buying high and selling low.

A long-term strategy is your game plan. It accounts for bad days, tough opponents, and unexpected conditions. It does not change because of one lost game or one hot stretch.

Efficiency Beats Excitement

The best players look boring when they win consistently.

They move well. They recover quickly. They make few mistakes. They put pressure on opponents without forcing outcomes.

Investing should feel the same way.

If your portfolio constantly needs attention, excitement, or adjustment, something is wrong. High-percentage investing minimizes decisions, controls emotions, and allows compounding to work quietly in the background.

Coach's Perspective

A coach would keep it simple.

"Stop going for winners too early."

"Build the point."

"Make them play one more ball."

"Trust your fundamentals."

"Win ugly if you have to."

The same advice applies financially.

What This Section Will Teach You

The chapters that follow will break down:

- How markets actually function, without jargon
- Why risk and return are inseparable
- How compounding rewards patience
- Why diversification beats hero ball
- How to think about investing as a system, not a series of bets

This is not about eliminating risk. It is about choosing the right risks at the right time and avoiding the ones that cost matches unnecessarily.

Winning the Point, Over and Over

You do not win tennis matches with one great shot.

You win by stacking good points.

You win by reducing errors.

You win by trusting your preparation.

Investing works the same way.

Construct the point. Stay disciplined. Let the opponent make mistakes. Over time, the score takes care of itself.

That is how high-percentage players win.

Chapter 9: How Financial Markets Really Work

Every tennis player remembers the first time the game felt fast.

The ball came off the opponent's racquet quicker than expected. Points were over before you felt settled. What looked chaotic from the sideline suddenly felt overwhelming inside the lines. But over time, something changed. The ball did not slow down. You did. You started recognizing patterns. You understood tendencies. You anticipated instead of reacting.

Financial markets work the same way.

To outsiders, markets look random. Prices move. Headlines scream. Opinions fly from every direction. It feels like guessing. But underneath the noise is structure. Once you understand how markets actually function, the chaos becomes manageable. Not predictable, but understandable.

How Markets Function

At their core, financial markets exist to connect people who need capital with people willing to provide it.

Companies raise money to grow. Governments borrow to fund projects. Investors supply that capital in exchange for ownership or repayment. Prices move based on expectations about the future, not just what is happening today.

In tennis terms, the market is the tour.

Different players have different styles, strengths, and weaknesses. Some dominate quickly. Others grind. Some fade. Some adapt and return stronger. The rankings change, but the system keeps moving.

Markets are not designed to feel comfortable. They are designed to function.

Trying to make them calm or predictable misses the point. Your job as an investor is not to control markets, just like your job as a player is not to control opponents. Your job is to play your game within the structure.

Stocks, Bonds, and Ownership

Understanding what you actually own matters.

Stocks represent ownership in a business. When you buy a stock, you own a piece of a company. You participate in its success and feel its struggles. Stock prices move because expectations change, but underneath that price is a real operation with employees, customers, and revenue.

Bonds are loans. You lend money to a company or government and receive interest in return. The upside is lower, but the predictability is higher.

In tennis terms, stocks are aggressive baseline shots. They push the point forward, but they come with risk. Bonds are rally balls. They keep you in the point and reduce errors.

You do not win matches with only winners or only rallies. You need both.

Investing is not betting. It is owning productive assets over time.

Market Cycles and Volatility

Markets move in cycles.

Expansion. Slowdown. Decline. Recovery. Repeat.

Volatility is movement, not failure. Prices going up and down feels uncomfortable, especially when values drop. But that movement is normal.

In tennis terms, volatility is momentum swings.

You can play a great set and still lose games. You can struggle early and still win the match. Momentum shifts do not mean the match is over. They test your discipline.

Investors who panic during volatility make the same mistake as players who abandon their game plan after losing one service game. They react emotionally instead of staying composed.

The market's job is not to move smoothly. Its job is to reflect changing conditions.

Long-Term Strategy vs Chasing Hot Streaks

Every tennis player has faced someone on a heater.

Shots are landing. Confidence is high. The temptation is to press. Swing harder. Go for more. Force winners.

That usually leads to errors.

In investing, hot stocks, trending sectors, and media hype create the same temptation. Chasing what just worked feels logical. It rarely is.

Long-term investing is about shot selection, not excitement. It is about taking high-percentage opportunities repeatedly, not forcing plays because of recent success.

In tennis terms, long-term strategy is constructing points. Chasing hot streaks is going for winners from bad positions. Sometimes it works. Over time, it costs matches.

Coach's Perspective

A coach would say it clearly.

"Stick to your patterns."

"Trust the game plan."

"Don't chase highlights."

"Make them beat you."

"Next point."

Markets reward discipline, not impatience.

Game Situations and Decision Points

The market drops sharply. Do you abandon your strategy or stay in the point?

You hear about a hot investment. Do you evaluate fit or chase momentum?

You feel behind financially. Do you press or stay patient?

These are point-by-point decisions. They compound over time.

Common Athlete Mistakes and Financial Parallels

Athletes press when momentum shifts.

Financially, that leads to panic selling.

Athletes chase winners instead of building points.

Financially, that leads to speculation.

Athletes abandon fundamentals under pressure.

Financially, that leads to inconsistent results.

Winning the Long Game

Markets reward ownership, patience, and discipline. You do not need to predict every move. You need to stay invested, manage risk, and let time work.

Tennis matches are not won by the most spectacular shots. They are won by players who make fewer mistakes and stay composed under pressure.

Financial markets work the same way.

Learn the structure. Respect volatility. Build a long-term strategy. Win one point at a time.

Athlete Takeaways

- Markets have structure, even when they feel chaotic
- Stocks drive growth, bonds provide stability, both matter
- Volatility is normal, not failure

- Chasing hot streaks leads to unforced errors
- Discipline and patience win long matches

Chapter 10: Risk, Return, and the Power of Compounding

Every tennis player learns this lesson the hard way.

You do not win matches by swinging as hard as possible on every ball. You win by choosing the right shots at the right time, accepting that some rallies will be long, and trusting that discipline eventually creates openings. Players who try to end points too early might look aggressive, but they also rack up unforced errors.

Money works the same way.

Risk, return, and compounding are not complicated ideas. They are misunderstood because people want fast results instead of trusting the process. This chapter is about learning how to manage risk intelligently, stay composed through volatility, and let time do the heavy lifting.

Risk and Reward Tradeoffs

There is no return without risk.

In tennis, stepping inside the baseline gives you more control and offensive opportunity, but it also exposes you if you miss. Hitting with margin reduces errors, but it may not finish the point. Every shot involves a tradeoff.

Investing works the same way.

Higher potential returns usually come with higher risk. Lower-risk investments tend to be more stable, but they grow more slowly. There is no investment that delivers high returns with no downside.

The goal is not to eliminate risk. The goal is to choose the right level of risk for your situation.

In tennis terms, this is shot selection. You do not go for the line on every ball. You adjust based on the score, your opponent, your conditioning, and the moment. Smart investing matches risk to your time horizon, income stability, and goals, not to hype or emotion.

Volatility vs Permanent Loss

This is where many athletes struggle financially.

Volatility is movement.

Permanent loss is damage.

Markets move up and down. Account values fluctuate. That movement feels uncomfortable, especially when numbers drop. But volatility alone does not mean something is broken.

Permanent loss happens when discipline breaks.

In tennis terms, volatility is losing a service game. Permanent loss is spiraling, rushing points, and dropping the set because you stopped trusting your fundamentals.

Selling during market declines, overextending with debt, or abandoning a long-term plan locks in damage. The market did not force the loss. The reaction did.

Athletes are conditioned to respond to discomfort. In investing, reacting emotionally often creates the very outcome you are trying to avoid.

Understanding this difference is critical. Feeling uncomfortable does not mean you are in danger. It means you are still in the match.

The Power of Compounding Over Time

Compounding is growth built on growth.

Your money earns returns.

Those returns earn returns.

Over time, the effect accelerates.

In tennis terms, this is daily drills and match reps. One practice does not change your ranking. Months and years of consistent training do. The work stacks.

Compounding rewards time, not intensity.

Starting earlier matters more than being perfect. Someone who invests consistently with average returns often outperforms someone who waits for the "right moment" or chases big wins later.

This is why patience matters more than precision.

You do not need to hit winners every point. You need to stay in the rally long enough for the advantage to show up.

The Cost of Waiting

Waiting feels safe.

Many people delay investing until they earn more, feel smarter, or believe conditions are better. The problem is that time does not pause while you wait.

Every year you delay is a year compounding cannot work for you. That lost time cannot be recovered.

In tennis terms, this is skipping training blocks and expecting peak performance later. You might still compete, but you are starting behind.

You do not need to start big.

You do need to start.

Consistency beats intensity. Always.

Coach's Perspective

A coach would not overcomplicate this.

"Play the percentages."

"Don't beat yourself."

"Stick to your patterns."

"Next point."

"Trust the work."

Risk is part of the game. The mistake is forcing shots or abandoning fundamentals.

Game Situations and Decision Points

The market drops. Do you stop investing or keep showing up?

You feel behind financially. Do you take reckless risks or stay disciplined?

You want to wait for the perfect moment. Do you start anyway?

Each decision is like a point. None decides the match alone. Together, they decide everything.

Common Athlete Mistakes and Financial Parallels

Athletes try to end points too early.

Financially, that leads to over-risking.

Athletes panic after momentum shifts.

Financially, that leads to selling low.

Athletes skip the boring work.

Financially, that leads to lost compounding.

Winning the Long Game

Compounding does not reward excitement.

It rewards consistency.

Staying invested through ups and downs. Choosing risk thoughtfully. Letting time do what effort cannot. That is how wealth is built.

Tennis matches are won by players who manage risk, stay composed, and trust the process. Financial independence works the same way.

One point at a time. One decision at a time. Over time, the advantage shows.

Athlete Takeaways

- Every shot has risk. Choose it intentionally
- Volatility is losing a game, not the match
- Permanent loss comes from abandoning discipline
- Compounding rewards time, not flash
- Starting early and staying consistent beats waiting

Chapter 11: Stocks Without the Highlight Reel

Every tennis player loves highlight shots.

The diving forehand pass. The running backhand down the line. The blistering winner on the run that brings the crowd to its feet. Those moments feel incredible, and they look even better on video. What highlights do not show are the missed shots, the poor decisions, and the unforced errors that quietly lost points earlier in the match.

Stocks are treated the same way.

People talk about the big winners. The stock that doubled. The company that "everyone knew was going to take off." Very little attention is paid to what owning stock actually means, how returns are truly generated, or why chasing excitement often leads to mistakes.

This chapter slows the game down.

What Owning Stock Actually Means

Buying a stock is not betting on a ticker symbol.

It is owning a piece of a real business.

When you buy stock, you become a partial owner of a company. That company sells products or services, pays employees, manages costs, and tries to grow profits over time. The stock price moves because expectations change, but underneath the price is a business doing real work every day.

In tennis terms, owning stock is committing to a match, not a single point.

You stay through momentum swings. You deal with good sets and bad sets. You accept that progress is uneven. Ownership requires patience, not constant action.

If you do not understand what the company does, how it makes money, or why it should exist long term, you are not investing. You are guessing. Guessing might win a point occasionally, but it is not a winning strategy over a full match.

Growth vs Value Investing

Stocks generally fall into different styles, with growth and value being the most discussed.

Growth investing focuses on companies expected to expand faster than average. These businesses often reinvest profits to grow. The potential upside is higher, but prices can be volatile because expectations are high.

Value investing focuses on companies that appear underpriced relative to fundamentals like earnings or assets. Growth may be slower, but stability is often higher.

Neither approach is right or wrong.

In tennis terms, growth stocks are aggressive baseline players. They dictate points, apply pressure, and go for openings. Value stocks are counterpunchers. They rely on discipline, consistency, and forcing errors.

Problems arise when you expect one style to behave like the other.

If you panic when a growth stock pulls back, you misunderstand its role. If you get bored with value stocks because they move slowly, you misunderstand theirs. Smart investors respect roles and build balance rather than bias.

Dividends and Total Return

Dividends confuse many athletes.

Dividends are cash payments companies make to shareholders. They are not free money. They are one part of the return you earn for owning a business.

Total return includes:

- Price changes
- Dividends received
- Reinvested earnings over time

In tennis terms, total return is the final match result.

A single great point does not win a match. Consistency, serve percentage, movement, and mental toughness matter just as much. Focusing only on dividends or only on price movement misses the bigger picture.

What matters is how everything works together over time.

Common Investing Myths

Several myths show up repeatedly, especially among competitive athletes.

Myth: Stocks are gambling

Reality: Ownership with discipline is investing. Guessing is gambling.

Myth: You need to pick winners

Reality: Consistent exposure and diversification matter more than finding the next star.

Myth: You must be aggressive to succeed

Reality: Patience and shot selection win more matches than raw power.

Myth: You can time the market

Reality: Most cannot, and trying usually leads to missed opportunities and mistakes.

These myths persist because they appeal to ego and emotion. Tennis teaches you quickly that fundamentals beat flash. Investing demands the same respect.

Coach's Perspective

A coach would strip this down to basics.

"Play your game."

"Stop going for highlights."

"Win the boring points."

"Make them earn it."

"Stay patient."

Great matches are rarely won with constant winners. They are won by players who manage risk, stay disciplined, and avoid beating themselves.

Stocks reward the same behavior.

Game Situations and Decision Points

You hear about a hot stock. Do you research the business or chase momentum?

A stock you own drops. Do you panic or reassess the fundamentals?

You feel bored with steady progress. Do you force action or stay disciplined?

These decisions feel small. Over years, they define results.

Common Athlete Mistakes and Financial Parallels

Athletes chase highlight shots.

Financially, that leads to hype investing.

Athletes abandon patterns under pressure.

Financially, that leads to buying high and selling low.

Athletes confuse confidence with control.

Financially, that leads to overconcentration and risk.

Winning the Long Game

Stocks reward ownership, patience, and understanding.

You do not need to be perfect. You need to stay disciplined, avoid emotional decisions, and let businesses do what they are designed to do over time.

Tennis matches are not won by the most spectacular shots. They are won by players who manage risk, control errors, and stay composed when momentum shifts.

Stocks work the same way.

Forget the highlight reel. Focus on the full match.

Athlete Takeaways

- Owning stock means owning a real business, not chasing a price
- Growth and value play different roles, respect both
- Dividends are part of total return, not a shortcut
- Most investing myths are just highlight-chasing in disguise
- Discipline and patience win long matches

Chapter 12: Bonds and Playing the Long Rally

Every tennis player understands the long rally.

It is not flashy. The crowd may not roar. There are no highlight-reel winners early in the point. Instead, it is about depth, placement, patience, and forcing the other player to miss. Long rallies wear opponents down. They stabilize matches. They change momentum quietly.

Bonds play that same role in investing.

They are not designed to steal headlines. They exist to provide structure, income, and balance so the rest of your portfolio can function properly under pressure. Athletes who dismiss bonds because they feel "boring" often misunderstand what wins matches over time.

This chapter explains why bonds matter, how they work, and when they belong in your game plan.

How Bonds Work

At their core, bonds are loans.

When you buy a bond, you are lending money to a government, a corporation, or another entity. In return, you are promised:

- Regular interest payments
- The return of your original principal at maturity, assuming no default

That is it. No mystery. No hidden trick.

In tennis terms, bonds are extended rallies cross-court. You are not trying to end the point quickly. You are keeping the ball in play, controlling tempo, and waiting for opportunities elsewhere.

Stocks represent ownership and growth potential. Bonds represent lending and income. They serve different purposes, just like offense and defense.

Understanding this distinction matters. If you expect bonds to behave like stocks, you will be disappointed. If you use bonds for what they are designed to do, they become incredibly valuable.

Interest Rate Risk and Credit Risk

Two main risks define bonds: interest rate risk and credit risk.

Interest rate risk refers to how bond prices react when interest rates change. When rates rise, existing bonds become less attractive, and their prices tend to fall. When rates fall, bond prices tend to rise.

Credit risk refers to the possibility that the borrower cannot repay the loan. Governments with strong finances generally carry lower credit risk. Companies with weaker balance sheets carry higher risk.

In tennis terms, these risks are like court conditions and opponent quality.

Interest rate risk is the surface. Clay plays slower than hard court. Conditions change how points unfold, even if your technique stays the same.

Credit risk is the opponent. Playing a top-ranked player is different from playing a qualifier. The risk of losing the point changes based on who is across the net.

Smart players adjust strategy. Smart investors adjust bond choices.

When Bonds Make Sense

Bonds are not about excitement. They are about purpose.

They tend to make the most sense when:

- You want stability
- You need predictable income
- You are closer to using the money
- You want to reduce overall volatility

In tennis terms, bonds show up when match management matters more than raw aggression.

Early in a career, you may play aggressively, accept more risk, and chase growth. As matches get longer, seasons pile up, and stakes rise, consistency becomes more important.

That does not mean you stop attacking. It means you choose your moments.

Bonds allow you to stay invested during tough markets. They provide income and balance so you are not forced into bad decisions at the worst possible time.

Stability in a Diversified Portfolio

Diversification is about combining assets that behave differently.

Stocks tend to fluctuate more. Bonds tend to fluctuate less. When combined correctly, they smooth the ride.

In tennis terms, this is having both offense and defense.

If your entire game is power, errors will cost you matches. If your entire game is defense, you will struggle to finish points. Balance wins.

Bonds reduce the emotional swings that cause investors to panic. They help you stick to the game plan when markets get loud and confidence wavers.

This is not theoretical. It is practical.

Most investing mistakes happen not because of bad math, but because of bad reactions. Bonds exist to help you stay composed.

Coach's Perspective

A coach would be direct.

"You don't win every point with a winner."

"Be patient."

"Make them play one more ball."

"Control the tempo."

"Stay in the rally."

Great players understand that not every point is an opportunity to attack. Bonds give your portfolio the same patience and control.

Game Situations and Decision Points

Markets fall sharply. Do you panic, or does your bond allocation give you confidence to stay invested?

You need money in a few years. Do you risk it all in stocks, or do you protect part of it with bonds?

Interest rates change. Do you overreact, or do you understand how your bonds are structured?

Each decision mirrors a match situation. You can force shots, or you can trust your rally tolerance.

Common Athlete Mistakes and Financial Parallels

Athletes hate boring drills.

Financially, they avoid bonds.

Athletes chase quick points.

Financially, they overexpose to risk.

Athletes underestimate endurance.

Financially, they ignore stability.

These mistakes feel small early. Over long seasons, they cost matches.

Winning the Long Game

Bonds are not about winning today's highlight.

They are about staying in the match when conditions get tough.

They allow your offensive assets to work without forcing you into emotional decisions. They protect against short-term needs derailing long-term plans.

Tennis teaches patience, discipline, and shot selection. Bonds reward the same traits.

You do not need to love long rallies. You just need to respect how often they decide matches.

Athlete Takeaways

- Bonds are loans, not ownership, and serve a different role than stocks
- Interest rate and credit risk are like court conditions and opponent quality
- Bonds matter most when stability and income are priorities
- Diversification balances offense and defense
- Long rallies quietly win matches over time

Chapter 13: Funds, ETFs, and Doubles-Style Investing

Singles tennis gets the spotlight, but anyone who has played doubles understands a deeper truth about winning.

You do not cover the entire court alone. You trust positioning. You rely on your partner. You communicate. You let the system do some of the work so you can play smarter, not harder.

Funds and ETFs work the same way in investing.

Instead of trying to pick individual winners and cover every angle yourself, you invest through structures designed to spread responsibility, reduce mistakes, and improve consistency over time. This chapter explains how mutual funds and ETFs work, why index strategies often outperform, how fees quietly erode results, and how diversification can be simple without being sloppy.

Mutual Funds vs ETFs

At a basic level, both mutual funds and ETFs are baskets of investments.

When you buy a fund, you are buying exposure to many stocks or bonds at once. That means instant diversification instead of relying on a single company or outcome.

The difference is how they trade and how they are managed.

Mutual funds are bought and sold once per day at the end-of-day price. You invest a dollar amount, not a share price. Many employer retirement plans use mutual funds because they are easy to automate.

ETFs trade throughout the day like stocks. You buy shares at market prices. They tend to be more tax-efficient and often have lower fees.

In tennis terms, mutual funds are structured practices. You show up, follow the plan, and let repetition do its job.

ETFs are match play. You see prices move throughout the day, but discipline matters because reacting to every swing leads to mistakes.

Both can work. The best choice depends on how you play the game, not on hype.

Index vs Active Strategies

This is where most investors get tripped up.

Active investing tries to beat the market by selecting specific securities. It relies on manager skill, timing, and decisions.

Index investing simply tracks a market or segment. It does not try to be smarter than the market. It tries to be consistent.

In tennis terms, active investing is trying to hit winners off every ball. Index investing is high-percentage tennis.

Active managers can win points. Some win matches. Very few win consistently over long careers, especially after fees.

Index strategies accept that markets are competitive, information is widely available, and mistakes cost more than patience. Over time, staying in position and reducing errors often beats chasing brilliance.

This does not mean active investing is wrong. It means you should understand the odds.

Most professional tennis players win more points by consistency than by flash. Investing works the same way.

Fees and Expense Ratios

Fees matter more than most athletes realize.

Every fund charges an expense ratio, which is the annual cost of managing the fund. That fee comes out quietly every year, regardless of performance.

A one percent fee may not sound like much. Over decades, it can cost hundreds of thousands of dollars.

In tennis terms, fees are unforced errors you do not see on the scoreboard immediately. They drain momentum point by point.

Lower fees give compounding more room to work. Higher fees demand higher performance just to break even.

This is not about cheap versus expensive. It is about value. If you pay higher fees, you should know exactly why and what you expect in return.

Most investors never ask that question.

Diversification Without Complexity

Diversification does not mean owning everything.

It means owning enough different assets so no single mistake ruins the match.

Funds and ETFs allow you to diversify across:

- Companies
- Industries
- Countries
- Asset types

All with one decision.

In tennis terms, this is court coverage. You position yourself so you can handle whatever comes back without scrambling.

Too many athletes overcomplicate investing because they think complexity equals sophistication. It does not.

Simple, well-diversified portfolios often outperform complicated ones because they are easier to maintain, easier to understand, and harder to abandon under pressure.

Consistency beats creativity when the season is long.

Coach's Perspective

A coach would be blunt.

"Stop trying to do everything yourself."

"Trust your partner."

"Play the percentages."

"Reduce errors."

"Stick to the game plan."

Funds and ETFs are not shortcuts. They are systems.

Great players respect systems because they know discipline wins when emotions rise.

Game Situations and Decision Points

You want exposure to the stock market. Do you pick a few names, or do you use a diversified fund?

You hear about a hot manager. Do you chase performance, or do you evaluate fees and consistency?

Markets get volatile. Do you abandon the strategy, or do you trust the structure you built?

Each choice mirrors a doubles point. You can overreach, or you can stay in position.

Common Athlete Mistakes and Financial Parallels

Athletes want control.

Financially, they overtrade.

Athletes chase highlights.

Financially, they chase performance.

Athletes underestimate small mistakes.
Financially, they ignore fees.
Athletes forget communication.
Financially, they abandon strategy.
These mistakes compound quietly.

Winning the Long Game

Funds and ETFs are not about brilliance. They are about staying competitive across seasons.

They reduce reliance on perfect timing. They lower the cost of mistakes. They allow compounding to do the heavy lifting while you focus on execution.

Doubles tennis teaches trust, positioning, and patience. Investing rewards the same qualities.

You do not need to hit winners every point. You need to stay in the match.

Athlete Takeaways

- Funds and ETFs provide diversification like a doubles partner covers the court
- Index strategies emphasize consistency over flash
- Fees are silent unforced errors that compound over time
- Simplicity makes discipline easier under pressure
- Winning over decades looks more like doubles than hero tennis

Chapter 14: Real Estate and Alternative Courts

Every tennis player knows the feeling of stepping onto an unfamiliar court.

The surface looks the same from a distance, but it plays differently. The bounce is higher or lower. The pace is faster or slower. Your timing is off for the first few games until you adjust.

Real estate and alternative investments are those different courts in the financial world.

They are not stocks. They do not move point by point. They reward patience, positioning, and understanding the surface you are playing on. For athletes, these investments are often appealing because they feel tangible, strategic, and "real." But without understanding the tradeoffs, they can create costly unforced errors.

This chapter breaks down renting versus owning, REITs and indirect ownership, alternative investments, and the liquidity and risk considerations that matter long term.

Renting vs Owning

Owning property carries emotional weight.

It feels like progress. Stability. A milestone. Many athletes are told that buying a home is automatically a smart financial move.

That is not always true.

Renting and owning are tools, not trophies.

In tennis terms, this is surface selection. You do not play the same style on clay as you do on grass. You choose the surface based on your game, your timing, and your season.

Renting offers flexibility. Lower upfront costs. Fewer surprises. It allows you to move quickly when careers change, income fluctuates, or opportunities arise.

Owning can build equity over time, but it comes with responsibilities. Maintenance. Taxes. Insurance. Transaction costs. Illiquidity.

Buying too early or stretching too far financially is like playing an aggressive style before your footwork is ready. It looks confident until the mistakes pile up.

The right question is not "Should I own?"

It is "Does owning fit my current match and season?"

REITs and Indirect Ownership

Many athletes like real estate but do not want toilets, tenants, or phone calls.

That is where **REITs** come in.

A Real Estate Investment Trust allows you to invest in real estate through publicly traded or private structures. You own a slice of many properties instead of one.

In tennis terms, REITs are practice courts.

You get exposure to the surface without committing your entire match to it.

REITs can provide income through dividends and diversification beyond stocks and bonds. They also allow liquidity. You can buy and sell many REITs easily, unlike physical property.

However, REITs still carry risk. They are sensitive to interest rates, economic cycles, and property-specific issues.

They are not "safe." They are simply different.

Indirect ownership is often a better starting point for athletes who want exposure without concentration risk.

Alternatives: Commodities and Private Investments

Alternatives sound exciting.

Commodities. Private equity. Private credit. Hedge funds. These investments often come wrapped in exclusivity and complexity.

In tennis terms, these are specialty courts.

They require experience. They reward discipline. They punish impatience.

Some alternatives can improve diversification. Others exist primarily to generate fees and mystique.

Common risks include:

- Lack of transparency
- High minimum investments
- Long lock-up periods
- Complex structures
- Limited regulation

Athletes are especially vulnerable here because sudden income creates access before experience catches up.

Just because you are invited does not mean you should play.

Alternatives should be used intentionally, in moderation, and only after core fundamentals are solid.

You do not experiment with trick shots in the middle of a tight match.

Liquidity and Risk Considerations

Liquidity matters more than athletes expect.

Liquidity is your ability to access money quickly without penalty.

Stocks and ETFs are highly liquid. Real estate and private investments are not.

In tennis terms, liquidity is recovery time. If you cannot reset quickly, you lose the next point.

Illiquid investments can create problems when:

- Income drops
- Injuries happen
- Career paths change
- Opportunities appear unexpectedly

Real estate and alternatives often look good on paper but feel very different when cash is needed.

Risk is not just volatility. It is also inflexibility.

A portfolio that looks strong but cannot move is vulnerable.

The Investing Concept Through Tennis

Real estate and alternatives are not about speed.

They are about positioning.

They reward patience, long horizons, and discipline. They punish emotional decisions and overconfidence.

Financially, this works the same way as adapting your game to the court.

You adjust strategy. You respect conditions. You do not force winners just because the crowd expects it.

Coach's Perspective

A coach would slow you down.

"Know the surface."

"Do not rush big decisions."

"Earn the right to expand your game."

"Protect your positioning."

"Stay flexible."

Great coaches understand that long matches are won by smart adjustments, not flashy shots.

Game Situations and Decision Points

You get a bonus or signing income. Do you rush into a property, or do you evaluate flexibility first?

You hear about a private deal. Do you ask about liquidity, fees, and lock-ups, or do you follow the crowd?

You want diversification. Do you overconcentrate in one asset, or do you spread exposure intentionally?

Each choice determines whether you control the point or chase it.

Common Athlete Mistakes and Financial Parallels

Athletes chase milestones.

Financially, they buy before they are ready.

Athletes underestimate recovery.

Financially, they ignore liquidity.

Athletes overvalue access.

Financially, they overpay for complexity.

Athletes trust confidence over fundamentals.

Financially, they skip due diligence.

These mistakes often show up years later.

Winning the Long Game

Real estate and alternative investments can play a role in long-term financial success.

But they are supplements, not substitutes, for solid fundamentals.

They work best when used patiently, intentionally, and within a balanced strategy.

Tennis rewards players who understand the court, manage risk, and stay composed over long matches.

Your financial life is the same.

Choose the right court. Respect the surface. Stay flexible.

Athlete Takeaways

- Renting and owning are tools, not trophies
- REITs offer real estate exposure without concentration risk
- Alternatives require experience, patience, and discipline
- Liquidity is a form of protection, not a weakness
- Winning long-term means adapting your strategy to the court

Part IV: Managing the Match

Championship players adjust without panic.

Every competitive tennis player has lived this moment.

The match plan was solid in warmups. Your strokes felt clean. The strategy made sense. Then the match starts, and something changes. The opponent adjusts. Conditions shift. Momentum swings. What worked early is no longer working the same way.

This is where matches are won or lost.

Not by who hits harder, but by who adapts without unraveling.

Managing your money works the same way. Early financial decisions are rarely permanent. Careers evolve. Income changes. Markets shift. Life introduces variables no one prepared you for. The difference between long-term success and long-term stress is not avoiding change, but responding to it intelligently.

This part of the book is about learning how to manage the match when conditions change, without panicking, overcorrecting, or abandoning the game plan.

Why Adjustments Matter More Than the Original Plan

In tennis, no serious player expects the original strategy to last untouched for an entire match.

You adjust grip pressure. Court position. Shot selection. Tempo. You respond to what is actually happening, not what you hoped would happen.

Financial plans are no different.

Your first budget, investment mix, or career strategy is a starting point, not a final answer. Rigid thinking creates more mistakes than flexibility ever will.

The goal is not perfection.

The goal is staying competitive point after point.

The Difference Between Smart Adjustments and Panic

There is a critical distinction every athlete understands.

Smart adjustments are intentional.

Panic adjustments are emotional.

In tennis terms, this is the difference between changing return position after noticing a pattern versus spraying winners after losing two points.

Financial panic shows up as:

- Selling investments after short-term losses
- Overreacting to headlines
- Making major changes without a clear reason
- Abandoning long-term plans because of short-term discomfort

Smart financial adjustments are slower, measured, and tied to real changes, not noise.

Championship players breathe, reset, and execute.

Momentum Is Real, But It Lies

Momentum feels powerful on court.

A few points swing your confidence. The crowd reacts. The match feels like it is slipping or surging. Experienced players know that momentum changes quickly and unpredictably.

Money has the same illusion.

Short-term performance feels meaningful, but it rarely reflects long-term outcomes. A good month does not mean you cracked the code. A bad quarter does not mean the plan is broken.

Managing the match means respecting momentum without letting it dictate your decisions.

You play the point in front of you, not the scoreboard.

Systems Replace Emotion

Elite players rely on systems.

Routines between points. Trusted shot patterns. Recovery habits. These systems prevent emotional decision-making when pressure rises.

Financial systems serve the same role.

Automatic contributions. Scheduled reviews. Clear rules for changes. Written plans that define when adjustments are allowed.

When systems are in place, emotion has less control.

You do not need to "feel confident" to do the right thing. The system carries you through.

Career and Life Transitions Are Match Conditions

In tennis, conditions matter.

Indoor versus outdoor. Heat. Wind. Surface speed. Ignoring conditions is not toughness, it is denial.

Life changes are financial conditions.

Job changes. Injuries. Family needs. Geographic moves. Income volatility. These moments require adjustment, not stubbornness.

Managing the match means recognizing when conditions change and responding intelligently, not pretending the court stayed the same.

Coach's Perspective

A coach would be calm and direct.

"Stay composed."

"Trust your fundamentals."

"Make small adjustments."

"Do not give away free points."

"Win the long rallies."

Great coaches do not chase emotions. They reinforce structure.

The Bigger Picture

This part of the book exists because most financial mistakes do not come from ignorance.

They come from panic.

From reacting instead of responding. From abandoning discipline under pressure. From confusing movement with progress.

Championship players do not need perfect matches. They need controlled ones.

Your financial life will never be static. That is not a flaw. That is the match.

Learn to manage it calmly, adjust intentionally, and trust the work you have already put in.

The players who do that are the ones still standing at the end.

Chapter 15: Asset Allocation and Court Positioning

Every tennis player learns this lesson early, whether they want to or not.

You can have great strokes, strong fitness, and confidence, but if your court positioning is wrong, you are always late. You reach instead of step. You defend instead of dictate. You turn manageable points into scramble mode simply because you are standing in the wrong place.

Asset allocation is court positioning for your money.

It is not about flashy shots. It is about where you place yourself before the ball is struck. When your positioning is right, the game slows down. When it is wrong, everything feels harder than it needs to be.

Opening Story: Standing Too Far Behind the Baseline

Picture a match where you start drifting deeper and deeper behind the baseline.

At first it feels safe. You have more time. You can swing freely. But soon you realize the cost. You give up angles. You lose offensive options. You let the opponent control tempo.

Nothing is "wrong" with your strokes. Your positioning is wrong.

Financially, asset allocation works the same way. Many people struggle not because they chose bad investments, but because their mix of investments does not match their situation, goals, or stage of life.

What Asset Allocation Really Means

Asset allocation is how you divide your money among different types of investments.

Stocks for growth.

Bonds for stability.

Cash for flexibility.

In tennis terms, this is your default court position. Are you aggressive? Defensive? Balanced? The answer should change depending on who you are, what match you are playing, and how long the match lasts.

Financially, this works the same way as adjusting your positioning based on the opponent, surface, and score.

Stocks, Bonds, and Cash: Knowing Your Tools

Stocks are your aggressive positioning.

They offer the highest long-term growth, but they also move the most. They are like stepping inside the baseline to take the ball early. Powerful when timed well. Uncomfortable if you panic.

Bonds are your stabilizers.

They dampen volatility and provide steadiness when markets get choppy. In tennis terms, bonds are retreating half a step when rallies get heavy. You stay in the point without overreaching.

Cash is your recovery space.

It does not grow much, but it gives you options. Cash allows you to respond without forcing shots. It is your ability to reset between points without stress.

The mistake is leaning entirely on one option. Too aggressive and errors pile up. Too defensive and you never pressure the opponent.

Domestic vs International Exposure: Playing More Than One Court

Many players grow up on one surface.

Hard courts. Clay. Grass. You feel comfortable where you trained. But elite players learn to compete everywhere.

Investing only in your home country is like refusing to play outside your favorite court. It feels familiar, but it limits opportunity.

International exposure spreads risk and expands opportunity. Different economies grow at different times. Different markets respond differently to global events.

In tennis terms, this is learning to slide on clay or adjust footwork on grass. You do not abandon your strengths. You expand them.

Diversification: Not Relying on One Shot

Every tennis coach repeats this relentlessly.

"You cannot win on one shot."

Even your best weapon needs support. When opponents neutralize it, you need alternatives.

Diversification is building a complete game. Different investments respond differently to conditions. Some perform well when others struggle. This is not about avoiding losses entirely. It is about avoiding catastrophic mistakes.

Financially, diversification works the same way as mixing spins, depths, and patterns. You reduce predictability and improve consistency.

Career-Stage Allocation: Adjusting as the Match Changes

No one plays the first set the same way they play the fifth.

Energy changes. Stakes change. Strategy evolves.

Your asset allocation should evolve too.

Early career is about growth. You have time. You can recover from volatility. You can afford to stand closer to the baseline and take calculated risks.

Mid-career is about balance. Income grows. Responsibilities increase. Mistakes carry more weight. Positioning becomes more measured.

Later career shifts toward defense and control. Protecting what you have built matters more than chasing every point.

The mistake athletes make financially is freezing their positioning. They play the same way at every stage and wonder why it stops working.

Coach's Perspective

A coach would simplify it.

"Know where you're standing."

"Adjust your position before the ball is hit."

"Don't overplay your hand."

"Win with balance."

"Play the long match."

Asset allocation is not a prediction tool. It is a discipline tool.

Game Situations and Decision Points

You are young and anxious about short-term losses.

Do you retreat too far and give up growth?

You experience a strong run.

Do you crowd the baseline and overextend?

Life changes. Income shifts.

Do you adjust positioning or keep standing in the wrong place?

Every decision reflects positioning.

Common Athlete Mistakes and Financial Parallels

Athletes chase offense at the wrong time.

Financially, that means taking too much risk.

Athletes play too safe when behind.

Financially, that means missing growth opportunities.

Athletes refuse to adjust positioning.

Financially, that means ignoring life-stage changes.

The problem is rarely effort. It is alignment.

Winning the Long Game

Great tennis players win by controlling space.

Great investors win by controlling allocation.

You do not need perfect positioning. You need appropriate positioning for the match you are playing. When your allocation matches your goals, timeline, and temperament, the game slows down. Decisions get easier. Pressure decreases.

Asset allocation is not about guessing where the ball will go.

It is about standing in the right place before it gets there.

Athlete Takeaways

- Court position matters more than swing speed
- Balance offense, defense, and recovery
- Do not rely on one shot or one market
- Adjust positioning as the match and career evolve
- Long matches are won by smart positioning, not panic

Chapter 16: Buying, Holding, and Trusting the Game Plan

Every tennis player knows this moment.

You walk onto the court with a clear plan. You studied film. You know your patterns. You understand what works against this opponent. Then two bad points happen. A missed forehand. A double fault. Suddenly doubt creeps in.

Do you abandon the plan, or do you trust it?

Buying, holding, and investing discipline is the financial version of sticking to your game plan when momentum swings. Most investing mistakes are not caused by lack of intelligence. They are caused by abandoning the plan under pressure.

Opening Story: The Match Plan Everyone Forgets

Before the match, the plan is simple.

High-percentage shots. Heavy topspin to the backhand. Long rallies. Make them play.

Then the match starts. The opponent hits a few winners. The crowd reacts. You feel behind, even if the score is close. You start going for lines too early. You rush points. You stop trusting what got you there.

That is how matches slip away.

Financially, this works the same way. Investors often know what they should do. The challenge is doing it when emotions are loud.

Opening and Funding Accounts: Getting on the Court

You cannot win points if you never step on the court.

Opening investment accounts is the financial equivalent of entering the match. Retirement accounts. Brokerage accounts. Employer plans. These are the courts where the game is played.

Many athletes delay this step because it feels technical or intimidating. But delaying is like warming up forever and never starting the match.

Funding the account matters just as much. An unfunded account is an empty court. The real work starts when money is consistently added, not when the account is opened.

In tennis terms, this is showing up to practice every day, not just buying new rackets.

Market Orders vs Limit Orders: Shot Selection Matters

Every shot has intent.

Sometimes you swing freely. Sometimes you place the ball with precision.

Market orders are aggressive and immediate. You buy at the current price. This is like stepping inside the baseline and taking the ball early. Fast. Decisive. You accept the conditions as they are.

Limit orders are more controlled. You set a specific price you are willing to pay. This is like waiting for the right ball before attacking. You are patient. You let the point come to you.

Neither approach is inherently right or wrong. The mistake is using the wrong shot for the situation or overthinking execution instead of focusing on consistency.

Long-term success comes from showing up repeatedly, not from perfect entry points.

Buy-and-Hold Discipline: Winning the Rally, Not the Highlight

Most points are not won with winners.

They are won because the other player misses first.

Buy-and-hold investing follows the same logic. You buy quality investments and give them time to work. You do not constantly change grip, swing, or strategy after every point.

In tennis terms, this is committing to rally tolerance. You trust your conditioning. You trust your patterns. You let mistakes happen without panic.

Financially, buy-and-hold discipline allows compounding to do the heavy lifting. The longer you stay in the rally, the more advantage shifts in your favor.

The biggest threat to this discipline is impatience.

Avoiding Emotional Decisions: Playing the Score, Not the Crowd

Tennis is emotional.

Momentum swings. Crowds react. Body language changes. The great players learn to manage emotion without suppressing it.

Investing requires the same skill.

Markets go up and down. Headlines scream urgency. Friends brag about hot streaks. Fear and greed pull at you constantly.

Emotional investing is chasing every loud moment. It is abandoning structure for reaction. It is changing strategy because of noise instead of data.

In tennis terms, this is playing the crowd instead of the scoreline.

The scoreboard matters. The plan matters. Everything else is distraction.

Why Most Investors Struggle With Holding

Holding sounds easy.

It is not.

Holding means sitting with discomfort. Watching volatility without reacting. Staying disciplined when others panic or brag.

Athletes struggle with this because sports condition you to react instantly. Adjust. Respond. Fix.

Money punishes overreaction. It rewards patience.

Financially, this works the same way as trusting your conditioning late in a match. You do not sprint every point. You trust the work you put in long before the match started.

Coach's Perspective

A coach would strip it down.

"Stick to the plan."

"Don't chase shots."

"High percentage tennis wins."

"Trust your preparation."

"Next point."

The same advice applies to investing.

Buying is not the hard part. Holding is.

Game Situations and Decision Points

The market drops suddenly.

Do you panic and sell, or stick to the plan?

A friend brags about a quick win.

Do you abandon discipline or stay consistent?

You feel bored because nothing dramatic is happening.

Do you force action or let time work?

Every choice reflects your discipline.

Common Athlete Mistakes and Financial Parallels

Athletes chase winners too early.

Financially, that means chasing hot investments.

Athletes abandon strategy after mistakes.

Financially, that means selling during downturns.

Athletes over-adjust.

Financially, that means excessive trading and fees.

The problem is rarely knowledge. It is emotional control.

Winning the Long Game

Championship matches are not won by one shot.

They are won by hundreds of disciplined decisions stacked together. Smart buying. Consistent funding. Patient holding. Emotional control.

When you trust the game plan, pressure decreases. Decisions simplify. Results improve over time.

You do not need perfect timing.

You need consistent execution.

Athlete Takeaways

- Enter the match by opening and funding accounts
- Shot selection matters, but consistency matters more
- Buy-and-hold is rally tolerance for money
- Ignore crowd noise and headlines
- Trust the game plan and win one point at a time

Chapter 17: Rebalancing and Momentum Shifts

Every tennis player has felt momentum change in a match.

You start strong. Your timing is clean. Your feet are active. Then something shifts. The opponent adjusts. Conditions change. Fatigue creeps in. Suddenly the match feels different, even if the score is still close.

The best players do not panic when momentum shifts. They recognize it, slow the match down, and make smart adjustments without abandoning their identity.

Rebalancing is the financial version of that skill.

Opening Story: When Momentum Turns Mid-Match

You come out executing your plan perfectly. Heavy crosscourt forehands. Consistent depth. You break early.

Then the opponent changes tactics. They start taking the ball earlier. They mix in slices. The rallies shorten. You lose a few games quickly.

Here is the critical moment.

Do you overhaul everything? New grip. New patterns. All-out aggression.

Or do you make measured adjustments while staying true to what works?

Matches are often lost not because momentum shifts, but because players overreact to it.

Investing works the same way.

How Often to Review Investments: Checking the Score, Not Staring at It

You do not check the scoreboard after every point.

You know the score, but you do not obsess over it. You check in at natural breaks. Changeovers. Set breaks. When something meaningful has changed.

Financial reviews should follow the same rhythm.

Daily monitoring creates anxiety. Monthly obsession creates noise. Long gaps create neglect.

Most long-term investors benefit from scheduled reviews, typically once or twice a year, with additional reviews when life changes occur. The purpose is awareness, not action.

In tennis terms, this is using changeovers to reset, hydrate, and refocus, not sprinting to the scoreboard after every rally.

What Rebalancing Actually Is

Over time, portfolios drift.

If stocks perform well, they take up more space. If bonds lag, they shrink. Cash levels change as contributions and withdrawals happen.

Rebalancing is the act of bringing your portfolio back to its intended mix.

It is not about predicting the future. It is about restoring balance.

In tennis terms, this is correcting court positioning. If you find yourself too far behind the baseline or crowding the net unnecessarily, you adjust. You do not redesign your entire game.

Rebalancing keeps risk aligned with your goals, not with recent performance.

Rebalancing Strategies: Making Small, Smart Adjustments

There are two common approaches to rebalancing.

One is time-based. You rebalance on a schedule, regardless of market conditions. This removes emotion and keeps discipline consistent.

The other is threshold-based. You rebalance when allocations drift beyond a certain range. This allows flexibility while still enforcing structure.

Both approaches work when applied consistently.

In tennis terms, this is adjusting based on either the set structure or specific patterns you are seeing. Either way, you stay intentional.

The mistake is rebalancing emotionally, reacting to headlines or short-term performance.

Life Changes and Portfolio Updates: Adjusting for New Conditions

Not all momentum shifts come from the opponent.

Sometimes the environment changes.

You move. You change jobs. You get married. You have kids. You experience injury or career transition. These life events change risk tolerance, time horizon, and cash needs.

Ignoring these changes is like playing the same strategy on a windy day, a slow court, or with a lingering injury.

Financial plans must evolve as life evolves.

Rebalancing during life changes is not market timing. It is strategy alignment.

Avoiding Over-Adjustment: The Danger of Chasing Control

One of the most common mistakes athletes make is over-adjusting.

You miss a forehand and change your grip. You lose a game and abandon your patterns. You feel pressure and start forcing shots.

Over-adjustment creates chaos.

Financially, this shows up as constant tinkering. Too many trades. Chasing performance. Moving money every time something feels uncomfortable.

This behavior feels productive, but it usually increases costs, taxes, and mistakes.

In tennis terms, this is trying to fix everything mid-rally.

Smart players adjust between points, not during swings.

Why Rebalancing Feels Counterintuitive

Rebalancing often requires doing the uncomfortable thing.

Selling what has done well. Adding to what has lagged.

This feels backward emotionally, but it is sound strategically.

In tennis terms, this is continuing to rally patiently when the opponent is swinging hard. You trust percentages over emotion.

Rebalancing enforces discipline when instincts push toward reaction.

Coach's Perspective

A coach would simplify it.

"Don't panic."

"Play your game."

"Make adjustments, not excuses."

"Stay balanced."

"Trust the process."

Rebalancing is not about brilliance. It is about control.

Game Situations and Decision Points

The market rallies strongly.

Do you let risk drift or restore balance?

The market drops sharply.

Do you panic or rebalance calmly?

Your life changes.

Do you update your plan or ignore it?

Every decision reflects whether you are managing momentum or being managed by it.

Common Athlete Mistakes and Financial Parallels

Athletes over-adjust after mistakes.

Financially, that leads to excessive trading.

Athletes chase momentum blindly.

Financially, that leads to buying high and selling low.

Athletes ignore changing conditions.

Financially, that leads to misaligned risk.

Discipline prevents overreaction.

Winning the Long Game

Great matches are not static.

Momentum shifts. Conditions change. Pressure builds. The winners are the players who adjust without losing identity.

Rebalancing does the same thing for your financial life.

It keeps risk aligned. It enforces discipline. It prevents small drifts from becoming big problems.

You do not need constant action.

You need intentional adjustments at the right moments.

Athlete Takeaways

- Review investments like you check the score, not every point
- Rebalancing restores balance, it does not predict outcomes
- Life changes require strategy updates
- Over-adjusting creates mistakes
- Stay disciplined when momentum shifts

Chapter 18: The Mental Side of Money

Pressure, Confidence, and Momentum

Tennis is never just physical.

At higher levels, everyone can hit forehands. Everyone can serve. Everyone can run. Matches are decided in the space between points. Confidence. Composure. Focus. The ability to manage pressure when the match tightens.

Money works the same way.

Most financial mistakes are not caused by a lack of knowledge. They are caused by emotion. Fear. Greed. Ego. Comparison. The mental side of money determines whether a solid plan is followed or abandoned at the worst possible moment.

Opening Story: Losing a Point You Should Have Won

You're up 40–15 on your serve.

You miss an easy first serve. No problem. Second serve goes in. The rally starts. You get a short ball. Plenty of time. You go for too much. Unforced error.

Next point, a little doubt creeps in. Another miss. Suddenly it's deuce.

Nothing physically changed. Your mechanics are the same. The opponent didn't suddenly get better.

What changed was your mental state.

Money decisions unravel the same way.

Pressure, Confidence, and Momentum

Pressure shows up in tennis when the score tightens. Break points. Set points. Tiebreakers. Confidence determines whether you swing freely or guide the ball.

Financial pressure appears during market downturns, career uncertainty, unexpected expenses, or big life transitions. Confidence determines whether you stick to the plan or abandon it.

Momentum can work for you or against you.

When markets rise, confidence can turn into overconfidence. When markets fall, pressure can turn into panic. Both lead to mistakes.

In tennis terms, this is the difference between playing aggressively within your patterns and swinging wildly because you feel unstoppable or threatened.

The goal is not to eliminate emotion. The goal is to prevent emotion from dictating decisions.

Crowd Noise and Comparison

Every tennis player hears the noise.

Parents. Coaches. Other players. Rankings. Social media. Someone always has an opinion. Someone always looks like they're doing better.

Financial markets have the same noise.

Headlines. Friends. Family. Online commentary. Social feeds filled with highlight reels of success. Everyone seems to be winning except you.

Comparison creates pressure that has nothing to do with your actual situation.

In tennis terms, this is changing your game plan because the crowd reacts, not because the strategy stopped working.

Your financial plan is personal. Different ages. Different incomes. Different goals. Different timelines.

Reacting to someone else's scoreboard is one of the fastest ways to lose your own match.

The Confidence Trap: When Things Are Going Well

Confidence is necessary to perform, but unchecked confidence becomes dangerous.

In tennis, overconfidence leads to lazy footwork, poor shot selection, and unnecessary risk. You stop respecting fundamentals because things feel easy.

Financially, overconfidence shows up during strong markets or income growth. You take on more risk than planned. You overspend. You assume good conditions will last.

Momentum feels permanent when you're inside it.

That is usually when discipline matters most.

Fear and Panic: After Lost Points

Fear shows up after mistakes.

In tennis, fear tightens swings. You push the ball. You stop trusting your stroke. You play not to lose instead of playing to win.

Financially, fear shows up during downturns. Market drops. Job uncertainty. Unexpected expenses. The instinct is to pull back, sell, or stop investing entirely.

Selling after losses is the financial version of guiding the ball into the net.

Lost points happen. Lost months happen. Lost years happen.

What matters is how you respond.

Building Systems for Discipline

Elite players do not rely on emotions to guide decisions.

They rely on systems.

Pre-match routines. Between-point rituals. Serve routines. Training plans. These systems keep behavior consistent regardless of mood.

Money requires the same structure.

Automatic savings.

Automatic investing.

Diversified portfolios.

Scheduled reviews.

Clear rules for when changes are allowed.

These systems remove emotion from execution.

If you rely on motivation, confidence, or "feeling good," you will eventually fail. Systems perform even when emotions fluctuate.

In tennis terms, this is trusting your routine when your legs feel heavy and the score is tight.

Staying Composed After Lost Points

Every match includes lost points that should not have been lost.

Double faults. Missed volleys. Poor decisions.

The best players reset immediately.

They do not replay the mistake. They do not rush the next point. They do not compound errors.

They step back. Adjust strings. Take a breath. Reset.

Financial mistakes will happen.

You will overspend at times. Miss opportunities. Make decisions you later question. Perfection is not the goal.

Compounding mistakes is the real danger.

Panic selling after losses. Abandoning saving after a bad month. Giving up on long-term goals because of short-term discomfort.

One bad point does not decide a match. One bad decision does not decide your financial future.

Coach's Perspective

A coach would not sugarcoat it.

"Control what you can control."

"Next point."

"Stick to the plan."

"Don't beat yourself."

"Stay composed."

Mental toughness is not about suppressing emotion. It is about executing fundamentals when emotion is loud.

Money rewards the same discipline.

Game Situations and Decision Points

Markets drop sharply.

Do you panic or stick to your system?

You see others posting wins.

Do you compare or stay focused on your match?

You make a financial mistake.

Do you spiral or reset?

Every response compounds.

Common Athlete Mistakes and Financial Parallels

Athletes play to the crowd.

Financially, that leads to comparison-driven decisions.

Athletes lose confidence after mistakes.

Financially, that leads to abandoning plans too early.

Athletes rely on emotion instead of routine.

Financially, that leads to inconsistency.

The mental game determines outcomes long before physical limits are reached.

Winning the Long Game

Tennis matches are not won by perfect play.

They are won by managing pressure better than the opponent.

Money works the same way.

You do not need to outsmart the market. You need to out-discipline your own reactions. Confidence matters. Patience matters. Composure matters.

The athletes who win financially are not the ones with the most excitement.

They are the ones who stay calm, stick to systems, and play one point at a time.

Athlete Takeaways

- Pressure exposes discipline gaps, not knowledge gaps
- Crowd noise creates bad shot selection
- Systems beat emotion when confidence fades
- Reset after mistakes instead of compounding them
- Win money the same way you win matches, one point at a time

Part V: The Long Season and Life Beyond the Court

M*atches are temporary. The career is the season.*

Tennis players understand seasons better than most people. A match is intense, emotional, and immediate. A season is quieter, longer, and harder to manage. You travel. You train. You recover. You lose matches you should not lose. You win matches you did not expect to win. What matters is not one result, but how you hold up over time.

Money works the same way.

Most people treat finances like isolated matches. A big purchase here. A market drop there. A raise. A setback. But financial success is not decided in any single moment. It is built across seasons.

This part of the book is about zooming out. It is about understanding how decisions compound across years, how life changes affect strategy, and how to stay disciplined when the structure of competition fades.

From Matches to Seasons

In tennis, players who only train for matches burn out quickly.

The best players train for seasons. They manage workloads. They plan travel. They prioritize recovery. They understand that pushing too hard at the wrong time shortens careers.

Financially, the same mistake shows up when people focus only on short-term outcomes.

Overspending after a good year.

Panic decisions after a bad month.

Ignoring long-term planning because today feels busy.

Those choices feel small in isolation. Over a season, they define outcomes.

The long season rewards consistency, not intensity.

Life Changes the Court Conditions

Tennis courts are not always the same.

Surface changes. Weather shifts. Altitude matters. Balls play differently. Players adjust strategy based on conditions.

Life does the same thing to money.

Career changes. Relationships. Children. Health. Aging parents. Income fluctuations. These changes alter risk tolerance, cash flow, and priorities.

Ignoring changing conditions is how players lose matches they should win.

Financial plans must adapt without being abandoned.

Adjusting strategy is not failure. It is professionalism.

Fatigue Is Real, Even Without Matches

One of the biggest surprises after competitive sports is mental fatigue.

Without a season schedule, travel plan, or competition calendar, discipline becomes optional. Decision fatigue creeps in. People delay planning because it feels exhausting rather than urgent.

In tennis terms, this is playing too many matches without proper recovery.

Financial fatigue shows up as avoidance.

Ignoring statements.

Postponing decisions.

Letting systems drift.

Hoping problems resolve themselves.

The long season requires rest, structure, and systems that operate even when motivation is low.

Income Is Not the Same as Stability

Many former athletes assume that once income improves, everything else falls into place.

In tennis, prize money does not equal career stability. Expenses rise. Travel costs add up. Injuries happen. Rankings fluctuate.

Financial stability comes from systems, not just earnings.

Savings.

Diversification.

Insurance.

Planning for taxes and retirement.

Income is offense. Stability is defense.

You need both to survive a long season.

Identity Beyond the Court

For many athletes, tennis provided identity, structure, and purpose.

When competition fades, those anchors loosen. Without intentional rebuilding, people drift. They chase status. Spend to feel successful. Compare themselves to others who look like they are winning.

The long season requires redefining success.

Flexibility.

Control over time.

Health.

Peace of mind.

Meaningful work and relationships.

These wins are quieter than trophies, but they last longer.

Playing Offense and Defense at the Same Time

Great tennis players know when to attack and when to rally.

They do not go for winners on every ball. They build points. Protect margins. Force errors.

Financially, this means balancing growth with protection.

Investing while managing risk.

Enjoying life while saving consistently.

Advancing careers while protecting health and relationships.

Overcommitting to offense creates fragility. Overcommitting to defense creates stagnation.

The long season rewards balance.

Coach's Perspective

A coach would remind you of the obvious truths.

"This is a long year."

"Take care of your body."

"Stick to the plan."

"Adjust when conditions change."

"Don't burn yourself out."

Money is no different.

You cannot sprint through decades.

Game Situations and Decision Points

Life gets busy.

Do you abandon systems or simplify them?

Income changes.

Do you adjust strategy or keep playing the same way?

Motivation fades.

Do you rely on discipline or wait for inspiration?

Season outcomes are shaped by how you answer these quietly.

Winning the Long Game

The long season is not glamorous.

It is steady. Repetitive. Often boring. That is why it works.

Financial success is not about dramatic wins. It is about staying healthy, staying disciplined, and staying in the game long enough for consistency to compound.

Tennis players who build careers think beyond matches.

Athletes who build financial security think beyond moments.

The court changes. The season continues.

The goal is not to win every point.

The goal is to still be standing at the end of the season with options, confidence, and control over what comes next.

Chapter 19: Taxes and Where You Place Your Shots

Every tennis player understands shot selection.

A short ball down the middle.

A wide forehand with the court open.

A low-percentage winner from behind the baseline.

Every shot counts as one point, but not every shot carries the same probability. Smart players do not just hit hard. They place the ball where it gives them the best chance to win the point.

Taxes work the same way.

It is not only about how much you earn or how well your investments perform. It is about where you place your financial shots. Two people can earn the same return and end up with very different outcomes based solely on how much they give back in taxes.

This chapter is about efficiency. Not avoidance. Not tricks. Just playing the court correctly.

Opening Story From the Court

Picture a long rally late in a match.

You are tired. Your opponent is tired. The court is open, but instead of moving them side to side, you keep hitting directly to them. The rally drags on. Eventually, you miss.

You did not lose because you lacked ability. You lost because of poor placement.

Financially, taxes work the same way. Many athletes work hard, save, and invest, but keep placing shots in the wrong part of the court. Over time, that inefficiency costs matches.

Taxable vs Tax-Advantaged Accounts

In tennis, not every part of the court plays the same.

Some areas give you margin. Others shrink it.

Taxable accounts are flexible. You can invest and access money at any time. The tradeoff is that taxes show up along the way. Interest, dividends, and capital gains can all create a tax bill.

Tax-advantaged accounts offer better efficiency, but with rules. Retirement accounts, health savings accounts, and similar vehicles allow money to grow with less tax drag, either now or later.

In tennis terms, taxable accounts are neutral rally balls. You can hit them anytime, but you do not get much margin.

Tax-advantaged accounts are high-percentage shots. You give up some flexibility, but you gain efficiency.

Winning players use both. The mistake is relying on only one part of the court.

Tax-Deferred vs Tax-Free Growth

Not all tax advantages work the same way.

Tax-deferred growth means you delay taxes until later. You may get a deduction now, but withdrawals are taxed in the future.

Tax-free growth means you pay taxes up front and withdraw later without tax, assuming the rules are followed.

Neither option is automatically better.

In tennis terms, this is choosing between playing aggressively early or setting up the point patiently. Both can win. Context matters.

Your income today.

Your expected income later.

Your career stage.

Your flexibility needs.

Good players read the scoreline before choosing shots. Good financial decisions require the same awareness.

Asset Location: Using the Court Correctly

Asset location is one of the most overlooked concepts in personal finance.

It is not about what you own.

It is about where you hold it.

Some investments generate more taxable income. Others are naturally more tax-efficient. Placing them in the right accounts improves after-tax results without changing risk.

In tennis terms, this is court positioning.

You do not hit heavy topspin shots from the doubles alley.

You do not play drop shots from ten feet behind the baseline.

You place the shot where it works best.

Asset location improves efficiency quietly. Over years, those small advantages compound.

Why Taxes Feel Confusing to Athletes

Taxes frustrate athletes for a reason.

They are invisible until they are not.

They arrive late.

They change with income, location, and timing.

Unlike a missed shot, you do not see the mistake immediately. The penalty shows up months or years later.

That delayed feedback leads to bad habits.

Ignoring taxes entirely.

Making decisions only at filing time.

Chasing deductions without understanding tradeoffs.

Reacting to headlines instead of personal context.

Taxes reward planning. They punish reaction.

Common Tax Mistakes Athletes Make

The same mistakes show up repeatedly.

Only using taxable accounts because they feel flexible.

Ignoring retirement and tax-advantaged options early.

Making investment decisions without considering after-tax results.

Waiting until April to think about strategy.

Letting convenience dictate shot selection.

In tennis terms, this is playing the same shot regardless of position or opponent.

It works sometimes. Over a season, it fails.

Coach's Perspective

A coach would not complicate this.

"Hit the right shot."

"Use the whole court."

"Do not force winners."

"Play percentage tennis."

"Win the long rallies."

Taxes are part of the match whether you like them or not. Smart players plan around them instead of pretending they are not there.

Game Situations and Decision Points

You earn more this year.

Do you adjust where you save, or just spend more?

You invest successfully.

Do you think about after-tax results or only headline returns?

The year is ending.

Do you plan ahead or scramble at the last minute?

Each decision is a shot. Placement matters.

Winning the Long Game

You cannot eliminate taxes.

You can manage them.

Just like tennis, the goal is not perfection. It is consistency and efficiency over time. Small improvements in shot placement win more points than occasional winners.

Athletes who learn to place financial shots intentionally keep more of what they earn, reduce stress, and build flexibility for the future.

You do not need to outsmart the game.

You need to play it correctly, one point at a time.

Athlete Takeaways

- Shot placement matters more than raw power, in tennis and taxes
- Taxable and tax-advantaged accounts serve different roles on the court
- Tax-deferred and tax-free growth depend on timing and scoreline
- Asset location improves efficiency without increasing risk
- Playing percentage tennis with taxes wins more points over the season

Chapter 20: Retirement Accounts and Financial Independence

Every tennis player trains for moments that are still far away.

You run drills in the offseason for matches you have not played yet.

You build endurance for third sets you hope you will need.

You practice patterns knowing they may not show up today, but they will matter later.

Retirement planning works the same way.

Financial independence is not about an age on a calendar. It is about options. It is the ability to choose how you spend your time without being forced by money. Retirement accounts are the long-term training tools designed to give you that freedom.

Opening Story From the Court

Think about a long tournament week.

Early rounds are manageable. You feel fresh. Recovery is easy. But as the week goes on, matches get longer and opponents get tougher. The players who prepared correctly still move well late in the match. The ones who relied only on talent fade.

They did not lose because they were less skilled. They lost because they did not train for endurance.

Retirement accounts exist for the same reason. They prepare you for the later rounds of life, when recovery time is longer and mistakes are harder to fix.

Employer Plans and Pensions

For many athletes, the first real retirement opportunity shows up through an employer.

401(k)s, 403(b)s, and similar plans allow you to invest directly from your paycheck. The most important feature is often the employer match.

That match is not a bonus.

It is not a perk.

It is compensation.

In tennis terms, an employer match is a free break of serve. You do not walk past it.

Automatic contributions matter just as much. Money goes in before you see it, which removes emotion and hesitation. That consistency is what builds endurance over time.

Pensions still exist in some careers. They function more like guaranteed income streams. While less common, they can play an important role in retirement planning when available.

The key principle is simple. If your employer helps you train for the long match, take advantage.

Traditional and Roth IRAs

IRAs give you options outside of employer plans.

Traditional IRAs generally offer tax-deferred growth. You may reduce taxes now, but withdrawals later are taxed.

Roth IRAs flip the equation. You pay taxes now, and qualified withdrawals later are tax-free.

Neither option is universally better.

In tennis terms, this is choosing between aggressive early play or patient baseline tennis. Both strategies can win. The right choice depends on context.

Your current income.

Your expected future income.

Your flexibility needs.

Your career trajectory.

Many athletes benefit from using both over time, creating balance and optionality.

Contribution Rules: Training Limits Exist for a Reason

Retirement accounts come with rules.

Contribution limits.

Income restrictions.

Eligibility requirements.

These rules are not punishments. They are structure.

In tennis terms, this is the practice schedule. You cannot train all day every day without breaking down. Limits protect long-term performance.

Understanding the rules helps you avoid penalties and missed opportunities. Ignoring them leads to unnecessary fouls.

Withdrawal Rules: Respect the Long Match

Retirement accounts are designed for later stages of life.

Early withdrawals often come with taxes and penalties. Those costs are the financial equivalent of an unforced error at a critical moment.

In tennis terms, this is going for a low-percentage winner when the rally is already in your favor.

Sometimes early access is necessary. Emergencies happen. But using retirement accounts casually breaks the long-term plan.

Discipline now creates freedom later.

Retirement Income Basics

Saving for retirement is only half the match.

The other half is how money is used.

Retirement income planning focuses on:

How much to withdraw

Which accounts to draw from first

How taxes are managed

How long assets need to last

In tennis terms, this is closing out a match.

You do not swing harder in the final game. You stay disciplined. You protect margin. You make your opponent play.

The goal is sustainability, not draining the account quickly.

Why Retirement Feels Abstract to Athletes

Athletes struggle with retirement planning because the feedback is delayed.

You do not feel the benefit today.

You do not see results next month.

The payoff is years away.

That distance makes it easy to delay.

In tennis terms, this is skipping conditioning because match day feels far away. It works early. It fails late.

Consistency matters more than intensity. Small contributions made early compound into powerful advantages over time.

Common Athlete Mistakes With Retirement Accounts

The same patterns show up again and again.

Delaying contributions because income feels uncertain.

Ignoring employer matches.

Only saving when it feels convenient.

Assuming there will be time later.

Confusing flexibility with freedom.

In tennis terms, this is relying on talent instead of training.

It works until it doesn't.

Coach's Perspective

A coach would keep it simple.

"Train for the long match."

"Take the free points."

"Be consistent."

"Don't cheat the work."

"Finish strong."

Retirement planning rewards the same habits that win matches. Discipline, patience, and repetition.

Game Situations and Decision Points

Your employer offers a match.

Do you take it or leave points on the table?

You qualify for an IRA.

Do you use it or delay again?

You want flexibility.

Do you plan ahead or hope future income solves everything?

Each decision is a rep. The reps add up.

Winning the Long Game

Financial independence is not built in one season.

It is built through steady training, year after year.

Retirement accounts are not exciting. They do not provide highlight reels. They quietly create options.

Athletes who respect the long match do not panic in the later sets. They stay composed, trust their preparation, and finish strong.

You do not need to know exactly how the match will play out.
You need to prepare so you are not forced to quit early.

Athlete Takeaways

- Retirement accounts are long-term training, not short-term results
- Employer matches are free breaks of serve
- Traditional and Roth IRAs are different strategies, not rivals
- Rules exist to protect endurance, not restrict freedom
- Consistent preparation wins the long match

Chapter 21: Housing and Major Financial Decisions

Every tennis player knows certain points matter more than others. A routine rally at 2–2 in the first set does not carry the same weight as break point late in the third. You do not rush those moments. You slow everything down. You check your position. You choose a high-percentage shot because one mistake can swing the entire match.

Housing decisions and major purchases are those points in your financial life.

They do not happen every month, but when they do, they shape everything that follows. One rushed decision can lock you into years of pressure. One patient decision can create stability and freedom.

Opening Story From the Court

Think about serving out a set.

You are up 5–4. The crowd gets louder. The temptation is to go big. Ace. Winner. End it fast.

But experienced players know better.

You raise your first-serve percentage. You aim for margin. You make your opponent play. You do not chase highlights. You protect the game.

Major financial decisions demand the same mindset. The goal is not excitement. The goal is control.

Renting vs Buying: Two Valid Shots

Renting and buying are tools, not identities.

Renting offers flexibility. Lower upfront costs. Easier exits. Fewer long-term commitments. It often makes sense early in a career, during transitions, or when income is unpredictable.

Buying offers stability. Potential appreciation. Forced savings through mortgage payments. It can make sense when income is steady and timelines are long.

In tennis terms, renting is rallying from the baseline. You stay light on your feet. You can change direction quickly.

Buying is stepping inside the court and taking control of the point. Powerful when timed correctly. Risky if forced too early.

The mistake is not renting or buying.

The mistake is buying because it feels like progress rather than because it fits your life.

Mortgages: Long Matches Require Endurance

A mortgage is long-term debt tied to a physical asset.

It is not just the monthly payment that matters. It is everything around it.

Property taxes.

Insurance.

Maintenance.

Repairs.

Time.

Stress.

In tennis terms, this is committing to a five-set match. You need conditioning, recovery, and margin. If your income is unstable or mobility matters, that commitment can become exhausting.

Down payments work the same way.

A larger down payment reduces pressure and monthly stress. A smaller down payment preserves cash and flexibility. Neither is universally right.

The right choice depends on your match conditions, not rules of thumb.

Cars, Leases, and Financing Traps

Cars are one of the most common financial mistakes athletes make.

They feel necessary.

They are easy to finance.

The payments seem manageable.

Until they are not.

Cars depreciate. Financing stretches payments over years. Leases lower monthly costs but restrict flexibility. Long loans reduce payments but increase total cost.

In tennis terms, this is going for a flashy winner from a bad position. It looks good for a moment. It hurts efficiency over time.

Transportation is a tool.

It is not a trophy.

If your car payment forces you to reduce saving, delay investing, or feel constant pressure, the shot selection was wrong.

Planning Major Purchases: Read the Scoreline

Big purchases deserve planning.

That means understanding the full cost, not just the monthly payment. Monthly payments hide reality.

Interest.

Opportunity cost.

Lost flexibility.

Increased stress.

In tennis terms, this is shot selection late in the match. You do not take a low-percentage shot if missing puts you in trouble.

A good rule of thumb is simple. If a purchase forces you to sacrifice emergency savings, retirement contributions, or sleep, it is too aggressive.

High-percentage shots win matches.

Why Athletes Struggle With Big Purchases

Athletes are used to structured progression.

Next level.

Better gear.

Bigger stages.

After sports, that mindset can quietly turn into lifestyle inflation.

Income increases. Spending follows. Decisions are justified because "I earned it."

In tennis terms, this is confusing momentum with control. Momentum feels good. Control wins matches.

Major purchases should support your life, not validate your identity.

Coach's Perspective

A coach would slow you down.

"Check the score."

"Play the point, not the crowd."

"Make them hit one more ball."

"Do not beat yourself."

"Protect margin."

Big decisions are not about aggression. They are about execution.

Game Situations and Decision Points

You feel pressure to buy a home.

Do you evaluate fit or chase status?

You qualify for financing.

Do you ask if you should take it or just if you can?

You want something now.

Do you consider the long match or just the next point?

The moment passes. The decision stays.

Common Athlete Mistakes and Financial Parallels

Athletes rush big points.

Financially, that leads to overcommitment.

Athletes chase highlights.

Financially, that leads to expensive purchases.

Athletes ignore recovery.

Financially, that leads to stress and burnout.

Most financial damage is self-inflicted through impatience.

Housing as a Strategic Decision

Housing should support:

Stability.

Flexibility.

Cash flow.

Peace of mind.

If it restricts career options, increases anxiety, or forces constant financial juggling, it is costing more than money.

In tennis terms, this is positioning. You want to be balanced, ready to move, and able to respond.

Winning the Long Match

Housing and major purchases do not determine success on their own.

But poor decisions here can make everything else harder.

The smartest players do not win by hitting the hardest. They win by making fewer mistakes. They choose high-percentage shots. They protect margin.

Financially, the same principle applies.

The best decision is often the one that keeps options open.

Athlete Takeaways

- Renting and buying are situational shots, not identity markers
- Mortgages require endurance, not just confidence
- Cars should support your game, not drain it
- Monthly payments hide true difficulty
- Patience and margin win the long match

Chapter 22: Your Career Is Your Longest Match

Every tennis player understands endurance.

A highlight winner might steal a point, but matches are won by the player who holds serve, manages momentum, and stays mentally engaged over hours, days, and seasons. The best players do not rely on one explosive moment. They win by staying solid point after point.

Your career works the same way.

Investments matter. Budgeting matters. Protection matters. But nothing impacts your long-term financial outcome more than your ability to earn, grow, and adapt over time. Your career is not a single tournament. It is the longest match you will ever play.

Opening Story From the Court

Think about a long three-set match.

The first set goes quickly. You feel great. Shots are clean. Confidence is high. But halfway through the second set, fatigue shows up. Conditions change. The opponent adjusts. Suddenly the match becomes about discipline, patience, and problem-solving.

The player who wins is rarely the one with the prettiest strokes. It is the one who manages energy, adapts strategy, and stays focused on the next point.

Careers unfold the same way. Early success does not guarantee long-term stability. Longevity comes from smart adjustments and consistent execution.

Salary vs Total Compensation: Reading the Full Scoreline

Salary is only one number on the scoreboard.

Total compensation includes everything around it.

Bonuses.

Benefits.

Retirement contributions.

Health insurance.

Paid time off.

Flexibility.

Career development.

Two jobs with the same salary can produce very different outcomes over time.

In tennis terms, salary is how hard you hit the ball. Total compensation is court position, recovery, and consistency. You cannot judge the match by one stat.

Many athletes make career decisions chasing the highest salary without understanding what they are giving up. Poor benefits, limited growth, and burnout quietly erode long-term value.

Smart professionals evaluate the full match, not just the opening set.

Job Changes: New Courts, New Conditions

Changing jobs is like switching playing surfaces.

New expectations.

New systems.

New teammates.

New benefits.

Each move resets the environment. Health insurance changes. Retirement plans change. Vesting schedules restart. Paid time off resets. Even stress levels shift.

In tennis terms, this is moving from clay to hard court. The fundamentals stay the same, but execution must adjust.

Job changes can accelerate growth when planned intentionally. Poorly timed moves create instability that spills into finances, relationships, and health.

The mistake former athletes often make is assuming effort alone will carry them. In professional environments, understanding the system matters as much as performance.

Negotiation Basics: Playing the Net, Not Avoiding It

Negotiation makes many people uncomfortable.

Former athletes often avoid it because it feels confrontational. But negotiation is not confrontation. It is communication.

You have negotiated your entire life.

Playing time.

Roles.

Scholarships.

Opportunities.

In tennis terms, negotiation is net play. You do not rush blindly. You move with purpose, understand positioning, and choose the right moment.

Preparation matters.

Know your value.

Understand the market.

Communicate clearly.

Small improvements in compensation compound over a career just like small breaks of serve compound over a match.

Avoiding negotiation is like refusing to move forward on short balls. You leave opportunities on the table.

Side Income and Entrepreneurship: Expanding Your Shot Selection

Side income can increase flexibility and resilience.

Coaching.

Consulting.

Content creation.

Business ownership.

These opportunities can supplement income and build skills. They can also introduce complexity, taxes, and risk.

In tennis terms, this is adding variety to your game. A reliable slice, drop shot, or net approach makes you harder to defend. Taking every creative shot without discipline creates unforced errors.

Side income should support your primary career, not distract from it. The goal is diversification, not chaos.

Many athletes chase side income because it feels exciting. Sustainable success comes from alignment and structure.

Why Athletes Undervalue Career Strategy

Athletes are trained to trust effort.

Show up.

Work hard.

Compete.

That works in sports. In careers, effort is necessary but insufficient.

Visibility matters.

Communication matters.

Timing matters.

Ignoring these realities slows income growth and increases frustration.

In tennis terms, this is hitting great shots without understanding score or positioning. You might look good, but you lose points you should win.

Coach's Perspective

A coach would be direct.

"Develop your game."

"Know your strengths."

"Play the long match."

"Do not give away free points."

"Earn every break."

Your career deserves the same intentional planning as your training.

Game Situations and Decision Points

You receive a job offer.

Do you evaluate total compensation or focus only on salary?

You feel underpaid.

Do you prepare and negotiate or stay silent and resentful?

You want side income.

Do you build it strategically or chase quick money?

Each decision shapes the match.

Common Athlete Mistakes and Financial Parallels

Athletes rely on talent alone.

Financially, that leads to stalled growth.

Athletes avoid uncomfortable conversations.

Financially, that leaves money and opportunity behind.

Athletes overtrain without recovery.

Financially, that leads to burnout.

Career missteps rarely show up immediately. They compound quietly.

Career Longevity and Financial Stability

Careers are built, not discovered.

Skills compound.

Relationships compound.

Reputation compounds.

Short-term wins mean little without sustainability. Former athletes who treat their career like a long match make better financial decisions because they protect income, flexibility, and optionality.

When income is stable and growing, everything else becomes easier.

Winning the Long Match

Your career is the engine behind your financial life.

Investments amplify it.

Savings protect it.

Insurance defends it.

But none of those work without a healthy engine.

The best players do not try to end the match in five shots. They trust their game, adjust when needed, and stay composed.

That is how long matches are won.

Athlete Takeaways

- Salary is one stat; total compensation is the full scoreline
- Job changes reset the court, not just the paycheck
- Negotiation is positioning, not confrontation
- Side income should expand your game, not create errors
- Treat your career like a long match and protect your endurance

Chapter 23: Estate Planning Basics Everyone Needs

Estate planning sounds like something for later.

Later in life.

Later in your career.

Later when things feel more settled.

That assumption causes more damage than almost any financial delay.

Estate planning is not about death. It is about control. It is about deciding who makes decisions, who receives assets, and how confusion is avoided when pressure shows up. Tennis players understand this intuitively. You do not wait until match point to decide your patterns, your go-to shots, or who you trust. You prepare in advance so the moment does not overwhelm you.

Estate planning is preparation for situations you hope never arrive, but must be ready for anyway.

Opening Story From the Court

Think about a tight third set.

You are serving at 5–5. The crowd is loud. Legs are tired. This is not the time to improvise. You fall back on patterns you practiced hundreds of times. Serve location. First-ball discipline. Clear decision-making.

If you have no plan, panic shows up.

Estate planning exists for the same reason. It removes guesswork when emotions run high and decisions matter most.

Wills and Trusts: Setting the Match Strategy

A will is the most basic estate planning document.

It outlines who receives your assets, who handles your affairs, and who makes decisions for minor children if applicable. Without a will, the state steps in. That process is slow, expensive, and impersonal. Your intentions may not matter.

In tennis terms, having no will is walking onto the court without a match plan. Someone else decides how the points are played.

A trust is a more advanced tool.

Trusts can provide privacy, efficiency, and control over how and when assets are distributed. They are not only for wealthy families. They are for people who want structure, clarity, and fewer surprises.

In tennis terms, a will is a basic strategy. A trust is a fully developed game plan that adjusts for different situations.

Both are better than chaos.

Beneficiaries and Account Titling: Who Gets the Ball

Many assets do not pass through a will.

Retirement accounts.

Life insurance policies.

Bank accounts with beneficiaries.

These assets pass based on beneficiary designations, not what your will says. If those forms are outdated or incorrect, your plan breaks down.

Account titling also matters.

Individual ownership.

Joint ownership.

Trust ownership.

Each structure affects access, taxes, and control.

In tennis terms, this is knowing who takes the next shot. If roles are unclear, hesitation creeps in and mistakes follow. Clear assignments keep the point clean.

Beneficiary mistakes are common, preventable, and expensive. Reviewing them regularly is one of the simplest ways to protect your plan.

Powers of Attorney: Having a Reliable Doubles Partner

A power of attorney allows someone to act on your behalf if you cannot.

There are two primary types.

Financial power of attorney allows someone to manage money, pay bills, and handle transactions.

Healthcare power of attorney allows someone to make medical decisions if you are unable.

Without these documents, loved ones may be unable to help you during illness or injury. Accounts get frozen. Decisions are delayed. Stress multiplies.

In tennis terms, this is playing doubles without a partner. The ball keeps coming, but no one is positioned to respond.

Choosing the right person matters. This is about trust, communication, and reliability, not emotion or obligation.

Healthcare Directives: Calling the Right Play Under Pressure

Healthcare directives outline your medical wishes.

They guide doctors and loved ones during serious situations. They remove guesswork. They reduce conflict.

These conversations are uncomfortable. Many people avoid them because they feel heavy. Avoidance does not protect anyone. Preparation does.

In tennis terms, this is practicing pressure drills. You prepare for tough moments so others are not guessing when it counts.

Clear directives protect your dignity and protect the people you care about from making impossible decisions without guidance.

Why Athletes Delay Estate Planning

Athletes delay estate planning for familiar reasons.

"I'm too young."

"I don't have enough yet."

"I'll handle it later."

These are the same excuses athletes use when skipping recovery, mobility, or film study. The consequences do not show up immediately. They show up later, when it is harder to fix.

Estate planning is not about predicting the future. It is about removing uncertainty.

Coach's Perspective

A coach would be blunt.

"Handle your business."

"Do not leave things to chance."

"Protect the team."

"Preparation is your responsibility."

Estate planning is not pessimism. It is professionalism.

Game Situations and Decision Points

You assume you are too young.

Do you delay or take control?

Your life changes. Marriage. Kids. New assets.

Do you update documents or ignore reality?

You want simplicity.

Do you create clarity now or confusion later?

Just like tennis, preparation determines outcomes.

Common Athlete Mistakes and Financial Parallels

Athletes avoid uncomfortable planning.

Financially, that leads to chaos.

Athletes assume someone else will handle it.

Financially, that leads to delays and conflict.

Athletes wait until problems appear.

Financially, that increases cost and stress.

Most estate problems are not caused by bad intentions. They are caused by inaction.

Estate Planning as Ongoing Match Management

Estate planning is not a one-time event.

Life changes require updates.

Marriage.

Divorce.

Children.

Career changes.

New assets.

Ignoring updates is like playing an entire season without adjusting strategy. What worked before may not fit now.

Regular reviews keep the plan aligned with reality.

Why Estate Planning Supports Financial Confidence

When estate planning is handled, mental bandwidth opens up.

You know decisions are covered.

You know roles are clear.

You know loved ones are protected.

That clarity supports better investing, better career decisions, and better life balance.

Confidence comes from preparation.

Winning the Long Match

Estate planning is not about the end of the match.

It is about controlling the match when conditions get difficult.

Clear instructions.

Right people.

Right timing.

That is how professionals protect what they build.

Athlete Takeaways

- Estate planning is about control, not age
- Wills and trusts set the match strategy before pressure hits
- Beneficiaries and titling decide who gets the next shot
- Powers of attorney provide backup when you cannot play
- Preparation removes stress from the people you care about

Chapter 24: Talking About Money With Family

Money conversations are rarely about money.

They are about expectations. Control. Fear. Guilt. Power. Love. Responsibility. Most families avoid them not because they do not matter, but because they feel uncomfortable. Tennis players understand this dynamic well. The hardest matches are not always against opponents. Sometimes they are internal battles. Nerves. Confidence. Doubt. Conversations with family about money work the same way.

Avoiding the conversation does not prevent mistakes. It guarantees confusion.

Opening Story From the Court

Think about a doubles match with no communication.

Both players want to win. Both care deeply. But no one calls balls. No one defines roles. One player covers the middle while the other backs up. Points are lost not because of lack of effort, but because of silence.

Money inside families breaks down the same way.

When expectations are not spoken, assumptions take over. When assumptions take over, resentment follows.

Talking about money is not about control. It is about coordination.

Teaching Kids About Money: Building Fundamentals Early

Tennis players do not start with match strategy.

They start with grips. Footwork. Swing paths. Reps. The basics are taught early so advanced concepts make sense later. Money works the same way with kids.

Teaching kids about money is not about numbers. It is about habits.

Spending. Saving. Delayed gratification. Choices. Tradeoffs.

Allowance, chores, part-time work, and goal-based saving are all reps. They teach kids that money is earned, finite, and purposeful. Shielding kids completely does not protect them. It delays learning.

In tennis terms, this is rallying before going for winners. You build consistency before power.

Parents who talk openly about money raise kids who are more confident and less anxious later. Silence creates mystery. Mystery creates mistakes.

College Students and Young Adults: Transitioning Responsibility

The jump from junior tennis to college competition is real.

Suddenly, you travel more. Manage your schedule. Handle pressure without constant oversight. Money works the same way for young adults.

College students and early-career adults face decisions about credit cards, rent, student loans, and spending freedom. Parents often struggle to know when to step in and when to step back.

The goal is not control. It is transition.

Clear conversations about budgets, expectations, and consequences matter more than lectures. Support without clarity creates dependency. Freedom without guidance creates mistakes.

In tennis terms, this is coaching from the stands instead of playing the point for them. Guidance matters. Ownership matters more.

Aging Parents and Caregiving: Reversing Roles With Respect

One of the hardest money conversations comes later.

Aging parents. Health changes. Care needs. Financial vulnerability.

This is where silence becomes dangerous.

Ignoring these conversations does not preserve dignity. It creates emergencies. Medical decisions. Housing changes. Financial shortfalls. These moments are emotionally charged and financially complex.

Talking early allows for planning.

Healthcare wishes.

Financial responsibilities.

Powers of attorney.

Care preferences.

In tennis terms, this is planning for long matches instead of assuming every set will be short. Endurance matters.

Approach these conversations with respect, not authority. This is about support, not takeover.

Family Expectations: The Hidden Scoreline

Every family has an unspoken scoreline.

Who helps whom.

Who pays for what.

Who is expected to contribute.

When expectations are not discussed, they turn into pressure.

Former athletes often become financial anchors without realizing it. Families assume success equals availability. Requests grow. Boundaries blur.

Money conversations help reset expectations before resentment builds.

In tennis terms, this is knowing the score before serving. You play differently at 40–15 than at deuce. Context matters.

Setting Boundaries Without Guilt

Boundaries are not selfish.

They are necessary.

Helping family financially should be intentional, not reactive. Clear limits protect relationships. Unclear generosity creates strain.

Boundaries might include:

What you can help with

What you cannot

When help is temporary

When help becomes harmful

In tennis terms, boundaries are court lines. Without them, every ball is debatable.

Saying no is not failure. It is discipline.

Why These Conversations Feel So Hard

Money carries emotion.

Pride. Shame. Fear. Obligation.

Athletes are used to direct feedback in sport. Family conversations are rarely that clean. They are layered with history.

The mistake is waiting for the perfect moment.

There is no perfect moment. There is only preparation and respect.

Coach's Perspective

A coach would frame it clearly.

"Communicate early."

"Do not let problems build."

"Handle it like a pro."

"Protect the relationship."

Avoiding tough conversations does not make you kind. It makes things harder later.

Game Situations and Decision Points

Your child wants financial help.
Do you teach skills or just write checks?
Your parents avoid planning.
Do you push respectfully or wait for crisis?
Family members expect support.
Do you clarify boundaries or absorb pressure?
Every choice sets precedent.

Common Athlete Mistakes and Financial Parallels

Athletes avoid hard conversations.
Financially, that leads to confusion.
Athletes try to fix everything themselves.
Financially, that leads to burnout.
Athletes ignore boundaries.
Financially, that damages relationships.

Building a Culture of Open Communication

Healthy families talk about money openly, calmly, and consistently.
Not in crisis.
Not in anger.
Not as leverage.
They treat money like training. Ongoing. Adjusted. Reviewed.
You do not need perfect language. You need honesty and respect.

Winning the Long Rally

Money conversations are rallies, not winners.
You do not force them.
You stay patient.

You keep the ball in play.

Families that communicate well around money experience less conflict, fewer surprises, and stronger trust.

That is the real win.

Athlete Takeaways

- Money conversations are about coordination, not control
- Teaching fundamentals early builds confidence later
- Transitions require guidance, not micromanagement
- Boundaries protect relationships and performance
- Open communication wins the long rally

Part VI: Winning the Match Over Time

Tennis is not won on one shot.

Not one ace.

Not one highlight winner.

Not even one great set.

Matches are won through accumulation. Point after point. Game after game. Set after set. The players who win consistently understand that success is not about forcing outcomes. It is about discipline, patience, and decision-making over time.

Money works the same way.

This final section is not about new techniques. It is about perspective. It is about zooming out and understanding how everything you have learned fits together across seasons, not moments. Winning financially is not about being perfect. It is about staying in the match long enough for preparation and consistency to matter.

The Difference Between Winning Points and Winning Matches

Every tennis player has hit great shots and still lost matches.

You can play brilliant points and still lose if you spray errors, lose focus, or let emotions swing momentum. Financially, the same thing happens. People make good decisions in isolation but struggle to sustain them over time.

A strong month does not build wealth.

A good year helps.

A disciplined decade changes everything.

Winning the match means managing energy, risk, and focus across the entire contest, not just early momentum.

Why Time Is the Ultimate Advantage

In tennis, time exposes habits.

Poor footwork shows up late.

Bad shot selection catches up.

Mental lapses get punished.

Money does the same thing. Time amplifies discipline and exposes shortcuts. Compounding rewards patience. Poor decisions do not always show up immediately, but they show up eventually.

Athletes understand delayed feedback. You do not see strength gains after one lift. You do not see endurance gains after one run. Financial progress follows the same pattern.

The player who stays disciplined when nothing seems to be happening is usually the one lifting the trophy.

Handling Momentum Swings Without Panic

Every match has momentum swings.

Bad calls. Missed opportunities. Runs by the opponent. Great players do not panic. They slow the match down. They return to fundamentals. They trust their training.

Financial markets behave the same way. Volatility is not failure. It is part of the match. The danger is not movement. The danger is reaction.

Selling in panic.

Chasing what just worked.

Abandoning a plan mid-match.

Winning over time requires emotional control more than brilliance.

Consistency Beats Intensity

Players who try to redline every point burn out.

They swing too hard.

They force winners.

They stop trusting patterns.

Financially, intensity without consistency leads to the same result. Overtrading. Overreacting. Overcomplicating. Sustainable success comes from repeatable habits.

Saving consistently.

Investing regularly.

Reviewing periodically.

Adjusting intentionally.

These are not exciting actions. They are effective ones.

Adjusting Without Losing Identity

Great players adjust tactics without losing identity.

They change targets.

They vary pace.

They manage risk.

But they do not abandon who they are.

Financially, your plan should evolve as your life changes. Career shifts. Family changes. Income changes. The core principles remain. Discipline. Balance. Long-term thinking.

Adaptation is not weakness. It is awareness.

Why Shortcuts Fail

Every player has seen it.

Someone chasing winners too early.

Someone skipping the grind.

Someone trying to out-talent preparation.

It works occasionally.

It fails eventually.

Money shortcuts follow the same arc. Speculation. Get-rich-quick ideas. Ignoring fundamentals. These strategies rely on luck, not process.

Process always wins over time.

The Role of Confidence Built on Preparation

Confidence in tennis comes from preparation.

You trust your patterns.

You trust your conditioning.

You trust your decision-making.

Financial confidence is built the same way. When systems are in place, decisions become easier. When protection exists, risk feels manageable. When plans are clear, noise loses power.

Confidence is not optimism. It is readiness.

Winning the Match That Never Really Ends

Financial success does not have a final whistle.

There is no last point.

No trophy ceremony.

No retirement from decisions.

There are phases. Seasons. Adjustments. The goal is not perfection. The goal is resilience and control over time.

Winning the match over time means staying disciplined when no one is watching and staying patient when results are slow.

That is how great players build careers.

That is how great financial outcomes are built.

Athlete Takeaways

- Matches are won through accumulation, not highlight shots
- Time rewards discipline and exposes shortcuts
- Momentum swings are normal; panic is optional
- Consistency beats intensity over long seasons
- Winning over time requires patience, preparation, and composure

Chapter 25: Advisors, Scams, and Long-Term Success

Every tennis player reaches a point where talent and effort alone are not enough.

Early on, you can win matches just by being fitter, faster, or more aggressive than your opponent. But eventually you hit a wall. The competition gets better. Matches get tighter. Small mistakes decide outcomes. That is usually when a coach enters the picture in a more serious way.

A good coach does not hit the ball for you. They do not play the match. They watch patterns. They see tendencies you cannot see mid-rally. They help you prepare, adjust, and avoid mistakes that cost you matches over time.

Money works the same way.

At some point, the game becomes complex enough that trying to do everything yourself, without guidance, creates unnecessary risk. Knowing when to get help, who to trust, and what to avoid becomes part of winning long term.

When to Seek Professional Help

In tennis, you do not wait until you are injured, burned out, or losing badly to get coaching. The smartest players bring in help before problems show up on the scoreboard.

Financially, the same principle applies.

You may benefit from professional guidance when:

- Your income increases or becomes inconsistent
- You start investing beyond basic accounts
- You experience a major life change like marriage, kids, or career shifts
- Taxes become confusing
- You want a long-term plan instead of guesswork

Seeking help is not weakness. It is preparation. The best players build teams around them. They do not try to be their own coach, trainer, and physio at the same time.

Types of Financial Advisors Explained Through Tennis

Not all advisors play the same role, just like not all coaches do.

Some advisors focus on investment management. Think of them as stroke technicians. They care deeply about mechanics and execution, sometimes at the expense of the bigger picture.

Some advisors focus on comprehensive planning. These are head coaches. They look at conditioning, strategy, matchups, and long-term development, not just one shot.

Some advisors are product-focused. They may resemble equipment reps. They can be helpful, but their incentives may not always align with your overall success.

Understanding how someone gets paid, what they focus on, and what they are responsible for matters. In tennis terms, you want to know whether someone is coaching your whole game or just selling you a new racket.

Recognizing Scams and Bad Advice

Every tennis player has seen shortcuts pitched as breakthroughs.

A new grip that guarantees power.

A drill that promises instant results.

A training method that ignores fundamentals.

Financial scams follow the same pattern.

They promise:

- High returns with low risk
- Urgency and exclusivity
- Complexity you are not supposed to question
- Emotional pressure instead of clear explanations

If it sounds like forcing winners every point, it probably ends in unforced errors.

Bad advice is not always illegal. Sometimes it is just misaligned. Advice that ignores your time horizon, risk tolerance, or personal situation can still hurt you even if it is technically allowed.

Good advice should feel boring, repeatable, and aligned with fundamentals.

Ten Common Financial Mistakes Athletes Make

1. **Chasing quick wins** instead of building consistency
2. **Ignoring defense**, such as insurance and emergency savings
3. **Overconfidence** after early success
4. **Following crowd noise** instead of a personal plan
5. **Not understanding fees**, which quietly drain returns
6. **Failing to plan for taxes**, turning wins into losses
7. **Letting lifestyle grow faster than income**
8. **Avoiding help too long**, then reacting too late
9. **Panic selling during downturns**

10. **No written plan**, just reacting point by point

These mistakes mirror tennis errors. Poor shot selection. Emotional swings. Abandoning strategy. The game punishes impatience.

Coach's Perspective: What Would Your Coach Say?

A coach would not sugarcoat this.

"Do your homework."

"Know who you're listening to."

"Stop forcing plays."

"Trust the process."

"Protect yourself first."

A coach would remind you that no one cares how flashy your approach looks if it does not work over time. Fundamentals win championships. Discipline wins seasons.

Financial discipline is no different.

Game Situations and Decision Points

Situation One:

You hear about a hot investment from friends who just made money. Do you chase it, or stick to your plan?

This mirrors deciding to go for a risky winner instead of rallying crosscourt. The smart play is usually patience.

Situation Two:

Your income increases. Do you upgrade everything immediately, or strengthen your base first?

This is like winning a few games and abandoning footwork. Early success does not mean fundamentals stop mattering.

Situation Three:

You face a market downturn. Do you panic and change everything, or adjust calmly?

Champions slow the match down when momentum shifts.

Ten Rules for Long-Term Success

1. Play defense before offense
2. Control what you can control
3. Keep costs low and discipline high
4. Build systems, not reactions
5. Stay invested through volatility
6. Match risk to your time horizon
7. Revisit the plan, not the emotions
8. Get help before mistakes compound
9. Stay patient when results feel slow
10. Trust the process over the noise

These rules are not exciting. Neither is footwork. But footwork wins matches.

Winning the Long Game

Long-term success is not about brilliance. It is about avoiding mistakes long enough for preparation and consistency to work.

Good advisors act like coaches. They guide, challenge, and protect you from yourself during emotional moments. Bad advice feels exciting. Good advice feels steady.

Just like tennis, money rewards players who respect fundamentals, manage emotions, and stay in the match.

Athlete Takeaways

- Get help before the match gets complicated
- Know who you're listening to and why
- Shortcuts and hype create unforced errors

- Discipline and defense win long seasons
- Trust the process, not the noise

Chapter 26: Losing the Schedule and Rebuilding Structure

Every tennis player knows the rhythm of a season.

Practice is scheduled. Conditioning is mandatory. Matches are on the calendar weeks in advance. You do not wake up wondering whether you will train today. The structure decides for you.

Then competition ends.

No coach is waiting. No court time is reserved. No one checks attendance. The calendar that once dictated discipline disappears overnight.

That is when life often gets harder, not easier.

Former players do not struggle because they forgot how to work. They struggle because the system that forced consistency is gone. Without structure, discipline becomes optional. And optional discipline is fragile.

Money is one of the first places where that breakdown shows up.

Why Life Gets Harder When No One Is Setting Your Calendar

In tennis, structure creates performance.

Warm-ups happen before hitting. Drills precede points. Recovery follows matches. The order matters. When the schedule disappears, most players do not immediately replace it. They assume motivation will carry them.

Financially, the same thing happens.

When no one sets deadlines, you can:

- Delay saving
- Skip budgeting
- Ignore account reviews
- Postpone planning

Nothing breaks immediately. That delay creates a false sense of safety. But just like skipping footwork drills, the cost shows up later, usually when it is harder to fix.

Structure removes decision fatigue. Without it, every good habit requires willpower. Willpower does not scale over time.

From Mandatory Workouts to Optional Discipline

Mandatory workouts eliminate debate.

You do not ask whether you feel like training. You show up because that is the rule. Optional discipline asks you to negotiate with yourself every day.

That negotiation is exhausting.

In tennis terms, this is the difference between a scheduled practice block and deciding to hit only when you feel sharp. Over time, optional reps turn into fewer reps. Fewer reps turn into rust.

Financial discipline works the same way.

If saving, investing, and reviewing money are optional, they are the first things sacrificed when life gets busy. The problem is not laziness. The problem is lack of structure.

Great players do not rely on motivation. They rely on systems.

How Lack of Structure Quietly Breaks Financial Habits

Bad financial outcomes rarely come from one big mistake. They come from small habits slipping quietly.

Miss one month of saving.

Skip reviewing a statement.

Ignore a budget for a few weeks.

Delay a contribution.

Individually, these feel harmless. Collectively, they change outcomes.

In tennis, this is missing recovery sessions. One skipped stretch does not cause injury. Repeated neglect does.

Without structure:

- Spending becomes reactive
- Saving becomes inconsistent
- Investing becomes emotional
- Planning becomes overwhelming

The longer this goes unchecked, the harder it is to restart. Momentum matters in money just like it does in matches.

Replacing Practice Schedules With Personal Systems

When formal structure disappears, it has to be rebuilt intentionally.

Elite tennis players who train independently still create structure. They block time. They track reps. They plan recovery. They do not wait for inspiration.

Financial systems work the same way.

Examples of personal systems include:

- Automatic transfers to savings and investments
- Monthly money check-ins on the calendar
- Annual planning reviews
- Rules for spending, saving, and investing decisions

These systems act like a coach setting practice times. They remove emotion from execution.

In tennis terms, this is trusting your routine before every serve. You do not reinvent it mid-match. You repeat it because it works.

The Investing Concept Explained Through Tennis

In tennis, consistency wins more matches than brilliance.

Financially, consistency beats intensity.

A player who trains three times a week for years outperforms the one who trains hard for two weeks and disappears. Money behaves the same way. Small, repeated actions compound. Sporadic effort does not.

Structure is what allows compounding to work. Without it, even good strategies fail due to inconsistent execution.

Coach's Perspective: What Would Your Coach Say?

A coach would not blame motivation.

They would say:

"Where is your routine?"

"Why are you freelancing?"

"Who is holding you accountable?"

"Trust the process."

"Discipline creates freedom."

A coach understands that talent without structure is wasted. Effort without systems burns out.

Money rewards the same mindset.

Game Situations and Decision Points

Situation One:

You get paid and plan to save what is left at the end of the month. Do you trust willpower or automate the transfer?

This mirrors deciding whether to warm up properly or just start hitting. Preparation wins.

Situation Two:

Markets feel volatile. Do you keep contributing or pause until things feel better?

Champions stick to the game plan even when momentum shifts.

Situation Three:

Life gets busy. Do you cancel your monthly financial check-in or protect it?

This is choosing between skipping practice or protecting court time. One choice compounds forward. The other compounds backward.

Common Athlete Mistakes and Financial Parallels

Athletes lose structure.

Financially, habits erode.

Athletes rely on motivation.

Financially, consistency breaks.

Athletes wait too long to rebuild systems.

Financially, mistakes compound quietly.

Athletes try to restart with intensity instead of routine.

Financially, they burn out again.

The fix is not harder effort. It is better structure.

Winning the Long Game

The most successful former athletes replace external structure with internal systems.

They stop asking, "Do I feel like it?"

They start asking, "What does the plan say?"

Money does not care about motivation. It responds to behavior repeated over time.

Rebuilding structure is not glamorous. Neither is footwork. But footwork wins matches.

The players who stay sharp long after competition ends are the ones who respect routines, protect habits, and keep showing up when no one is watching.

Athlete Takeaways

- Structure beats motivation every time
- Optional discipline fades without systems
- Small habits slipping quietly change outcomes
- Build routines you can repeat under stress
- Consistency wins long matches and long careers

Chapter 27: From Teammates to Coworkers

Think about your time on a tennis team.

Even in an individual sport, the structure is clear. Coaches run practice. Lineups matter. Roles are defined. Feedback is constant. Film, stats, and rankings tell you exactly where you stand. You know who makes decisions and how performance is measured.

Then tennis ends, and you walk into the workplace.

Suddenly, none of that clarity exists.

There is no coach standing on the sideline. No ranking posted on the wall. No clear scoreline telling you whether you are winning or losing. You are surrounded by coworkers instead of teammates, and the rules feel unspoken.

For many former athletes, this transition is more disorienting than they expect. Not because they lack work ethic or discipline, but because the environment has fundamentally changed.

Why the Workplace Feels Foreign After Sports

Sports environments are designed for clarity.

You practice to compete. You compete to win. Performance is visible. Effort is obvious. Accountability is built into the system.

Workplaces are different.

Performance metrics are often vague. Expectations are implied rather than stated. Promotions are not always tied directly to output. Recognition can depend as much on perception as production.

For athletes used to clean feedback loops, this can feel unfair or confusing.

In tennis terms, this is like playing a match where the score is not displayed and the rules change mid-set. You are still expected to compete, but you are not always sure what the umpire is watching.

Authority Without Coaches

In tennis, authority is obvious.

The head coach sets the plan. Assistants reinforce it. Captains help maintain standards. You may not like every decision, but you know who makes them.

In the workplace, authority is often indirect.

Titles do not always reflect influence. Some managers avoid confrontation. Decisions may happen behind closed doors. Power can sit with people who are not the most visible.

Former athletes often struggle here because they wait for direction.

They expect:

- Clear instructions
- Direct feedback
- Defined expectations

When those do not come, they hesitate. That hesitation can be misread as lack of initiative.

In tennis terms, this is waiting for your coach to call a play during a point. At some level, you are expected to read the court and adjust on your own.

Feedback Without Film

Athletes live on feedback.

You watch film. You review mistakes. You get corrections in real time. If something is not working, someone tells you.

In the workplace, feedback is inconsistent.

You may hear nothing for months. Reviews may be annual. Criticism is often softened or avoided entirely. Praise can be vague.

The danger is not harsh feedback. The danger is silence.

Without feedback, you may assume you are doing fine until a missed promotion, stalled raise, or unexpected termination proves otherwise.

In tennis terms, this is playing match after match without reviewing tape, then being told at the end of the season that your footwork has been hurting you all year.

Former athletes must learn to ask for feedback instead of waiting for it.

Politics, Ambiguity, and Unclear Expectations

Sports reward performance first.

Workplaces reward performance, relationships, timing, and perception.

This reality makes many former athletes uncomfortable. They were taught that effort and results speak for themselves. In business, effort still matters, but it is not always visible unless you communicate it.

Politics does not mean dishonesty. It means understanding how decisions are made, who influences them, and how your work is perceived.

Ignoring politics does not make them disappear. It just means you are playing without awareness.

In tennis terms, this is refusing to adjust your strategy based on an opponent's tendencies. You may hit great shots, but you will lose if you ignore the context.

How This Impacts Income Growth and Career Stability

Confusion slows progress.

When expectations are unclear, you may:

- Work hard on the wrong things
- Miss opportunities to advocate for yourself

- Stay too long in roles that do not reward growth
- Change jobs out of frustration instead of strategy

Income growth depends on alignment. You need to understand what is valued, who decides, and how to position yourself.

Former athletes who adapt tend to grow faster. They:

- Ask questions
- Seek clarity
- Build relationships
- Communicate progress
- Take ownership of their development

Those who do not often feel stuck, underpaid, or overlooked despite strong effort.

The Investing Concept Explained Through Tennis

In tennis, winning is not just about hitting harder.

It is about reading the match, adjusting strategy, managing momentum, and understanding how points are actually won.

Careers work the same way.

You cannot assume the workplace rewards the same things sports did. You have to learn the system, then compete within it.

Financially, income growth is your primary engine. If career confusion limits income, every other financial goal becomes harder.

Understanding the workplace is part of your financial strategy.

Coach's Perspective: What Would Your Coach Say?

A coach would not sugarcoat it.

They would say:

"Learn the system."

"Ask questions."

"Stop waiting to be told."

"Control what you can control."

"Advocate for yourself."

"Do not confuse silence with approval."

A good coach knows that talent alone does not guarantee playing time. Awareness, communication, and adaptability matter.

The workplace is no different.

Game Situations and Decision Points

Situation One:

You are unsure what your manager values most. Do you guess and hope, or do you ask directly?

That is the difference between guessing shot selection and scouting an opponent.

Situation Two:

You want a raise or promotion. Do you wait to be noticed, or do you prepare a case and advocate?

This mirrors waiting for points versus creating them.

Situation Three:

You feel frustrated by office politics. Do you disengage, or do you learn how to navigate professionally?

That choice determines whether you grow or stall.

Common Athlete Mistakes and Financial Parallels

Athletes wait for direction.

Financially, income growth stalls.

Athletes avoid politics entirely.

Financially, opportunities shrink.

Athletes expect fairness without communication.

Financially, frustration builds.

Athletes confuse effort with visibility.

Financially, contributions go unnoticed.

Awareness changes outcomes.

Winning the Long Game

The workplace is not the locker room.

The rules are different. The scoreboard is hidden. The feedback loop is slower.

But success is still possible.

Former athletes who thrive do not abandon their discipline. They adapt it. They replace coaches with mentors. Film with feedback conversations. Playbooks with personal career plans.

They learn how the game is actually played, then execute with patience and professionalism.

Your career is one of the longest matches you will ever play. Learning how coworkers, managers, and systems operate is part of staying in the match.

Athlete Takeaways

- The workplace rewards awareness, not just effort
- Authority and feedback are less obvious than in sports
- Communication protects income growth
- Waiting for direction limits opportunity
- Learn the system, then compete within it

Chapter 28: When No One Is Watching Anymore

Think about a long practice session when no matches were scheduled.

No crowd.

No rankings on the line.

No opponent across the net.

Just you, a basket of balls, and a court that would expose how much discipline you really had.

Some days, you stayed locked in. You worked on footwork, consistency, and patterns. Other days, the reps slipped. Breaks got longer. Focus drifted. Nobody blew a whistle. Nobody called you out. The difference showed up weeks later when matches mattered.

Life after tennis feels exactly like that.

When competition ends, accountability fades. No coach sets your schedule. No one tracks reps. No one notices if you skip the basics. The pressure that once sharpened habits quietly disappears, and many former athletes struggle not because they lost discipline, but because the environment that enforced it is gone.

The Discipline Gap After Accountability Disappears

In tennis, accountability is constant.

If you skip conditioning, your legs fail late in sets. If you neglect serves, double faults show up under pressure. Structure forces discipline because consequences are immediate.

After sports, accountability becomes internal.

You can skip budgeting. Delay saving. Ignore planning. Nothing bad happens right away. Bills still get paid. Life continues. That delay is what makes it dangerous.

In tennis terms, this is rallying casually instead of practicing with intention. You feel fine in the moment, but your edge erodes quietly.

This gap between knowing what to do and consistently doing it is where many former athletes struggle financially.

Why Former Athletes Self-Sabotage Without Pressure

Pressure sharpens focus.

Matches create urgency. Scorelines demand execution. Without pressure, comfort sneaks in.

Netflix replaces workouts.

Spending replaces saving.

Convenience replaces planning.

This is not laziness. It is human nature. Athletes are trained in high-accountability environments. When that structure disappears, many struggle to generate urgency on their own.

In tennis terms, this is practicing without targets. You still hit balls, but nothing is pushing you to improve.

Self-sabotage rarely looks dramatic. It looks like drift.

Comfort vs Growth Decisions

Every decision falls somewhere between comfort and growth.

Comfort feels good now. Growth feels uncomfortable now but pays off later.

In tennis, comfort is rallying safely down the middle instead of working on weaker shots. Growth is practicing the uncomfortable patterns that make you better under pressure.

Financially, comfort shows up as:

- Spending instead of saving
- Avoiding difficult conversations
- Ignoring long-term planning
- Choosing ease over discipline

Growth shows up as:

- Automating savings
- Saying no to lifestyle inflation
- Reviewing finances regularly
- Making decisions that future you will thank you for

The danger is not one comfort decision. It is choosing comfort repeatedly.

Translating "Grind Culture" Into Adult Life

Many athletes try to replace structure with grind.

They work longer hours. Push harder. Chase intensity. That works in short bursts but fails long-term.

Adult life rewards systems, not constant effort.

You do not get points for exhaustion. You get results from consistency.

In tennis terms, this is swinging harder instead of improving footwork. It feels productive but leads to errors and burnout.

Sustainable discipline looks like:

- Automatic contributions
- Simple rules that remove decision-making
- Regular check-ins instead of constant stress
- Building habits that work even on low-motivation days

Grind culture burns out without structure. Systems create freedom.

Why Money Mistakes Show Up Years Later

Money is delayed feedback.

Overspending today does not hurt tomorrow. Skipping saving does not hurt this month. Poor decisions compound quietly.

The consequences show up years later as:

- Limited options
- Career pressure
- Anxiety about retirement
- Feeling behind without knowing why

In tennis terms, this is neglecting conditioning early in the season. You do not feel it until the third set, when your legs disappear.

Most financial mistakes are not catastrophic. They are cumulative.

The Investing Concept Explained Through Tennis

In tennis, winning is not about one highlight shot.

It is about point construction. Shot selection. Mental discipline. Repeating high-percentage plays over and over.

Money works the same way.

You do not win financially by making one big move. You win by consistently making smart, boring decisions when no one is watching.

Discipline in private creates results in public.

Coach's Perspective: What Would Your Coach Say?

A coach would be blunt.

"Nobody is watching right now."

"That does not mean it does not matter."

"Control what you can control."

"Next point."

"Do not beat yourself."

"Champions are built when nobody's watching."

A good coach knows habits form in quiet moments. Matches only reveal what was already built.

Your financial life is no different.

Game Situations and Decision Points

Situation One:

You are tired after work. Do you skip reviewing your finances again, or do you stick to the routine?

That choice mirrors practicing when energy is low.

Situation Two:

No one will notice if you overspend this month. Do you choose comfort or discipline?

That mirrors playing safely versus improving your weaknesses.

Situation Three:

The payoff feels far away. Do you stay consistent or abandon the plan?

That mirrors trusting training before results show up.

What you do when no one is watching defines outcomes.

Common Athlete Mistakes and Financial Parallels

Athletes rely on external accountability.

Financially, habits drift.

Athletes chase comfort when pressure disappears.

Financially, saving slows and spending grows.

Athletes confuse grind with progress.

Financially, burnout replaces consistency.

Athletes underestimate delayed consequences.

Financially, regret arrives years later.

Awareness closes the gap.

Winning the Long Game

Discipline without an audience is harder, but it is more powerful.

The habits you maintain privately shape the results you see publicly. Financial stability is not built during windfalls or big moments. It is built in quiet, boring consistency.

Former athletes who thrive replace coaches with systems. They replace schedules with routines. They replace pressure with purpose.

You do not need perfection.

You need persistence.

Athlete Takeaways

- Accountability disappears after tennis
- Discipline must become internal
- Comfort choices compound into problems
- Systems beat grind culture
- What you do when no one is watching decides the match

Chapter 29: Redefining Winning After the Uniform Comes Off

Think about a tight match where the scoreline is close, but something feels off.

You might be up a break, but you are forcing shots. Going for winners too early. Playing for how the point looks instead of how it is built. The crowd reacts, but inside, you know you are not playing your best tennis.

Eventually, that catches up to you.

Life after tennis creates a similar tension.

For most of your playing career, winning was clearly defined. Points. Games. Sets. Rankings. Trophies. You always knew the score. When the uniform comes off, that clarity disappears. The competitive instinct stays, but the scoreboard is gone. Many former athletes fill that gap with the wrong metrics without realizing it.

Why Chasing Status Replaces Chasing Performance

Tennis rewards performance.

You win points by executing patterns, managing risk, and staying disciplined. Life, however, often rewards appearance.

Without a clear scoreboard, people default to visible markers of success. Income. Titles. Houses. Cars. Social media signals. These things look like winning, even when they do not feel like it.

In tennis terms, this is swinging for highlight winners instead of constructing points.

Status creates short-term validation. Performance creates long-term fulfillment.

Former athletes are especially vulnerable to this shift because they are wired to compete. When performance is no longer clearly measured, comparison replaces mastery.

Income vs Fulfillment

Income matters.

It provides stability, options, and security. But income alone does not create satisfaction.

Many former athletes hit financial milestones and still feel restless. The structure is gone. The feedback is gone. The sense of progress feels muted.

In tennis terms, this is winning a match while playing sloppy tennis. The result counts, but it does not feel right.

Fulfillment comes from alignment. Growth. Contribution. Control over time. Feeling that your daily effort matches your values. Income supports those things. It does not replace them.

When income becomes the only scoreboard, decision-making suffers. People stay in roles they dislike. Take on unnecessary pressure. Spend to signal success instead of building it.

Titles, Houses, Cars, and Comparison Traps

Comparison is constant.

Former teammates become measuring sticks. Social media amplifies it. You see promotions, lifestyles, and milestones without context.

Comparison creates urgency that is not yours.

In tennis terms, this is changing your game plan because the opponent hit one flashy shot. You abandon your strategy and start forcing points.

Big houses, luxury cars, and impressive titles are not inherently bad. The problem is chasing them as proof of worth.

There is always someone with more. Bigger contracts. Nicer homes. Flashier lifestyles. If comparison drives your definition of winning, the finish line keeps moving.

That pressure leads to overspending, burnout, and regret.

What "Success" Actually Looks Like in Your 30s and 40s

Success evolves.

In your 30s and 40s, winning often looks quieter:

- Flexibility in your schedule
- Financial stability without anxiety
- Health and energy
- Time with people who matter
- Work that aligns with your values
- Options instead of obligations

These wins do not show up on a highlight reel.

In tennis terms, this is winning matches by controlling tempo, managing energy, and minimizing errors. It is not flashy, but it is effective.

Former athletes who redefine success early make better decisions. They stop chasing external validation and start building lives that feel sustainable.

Building a New Scoreboard

You cannot win a match if you do not know the score.

After sports, you have to build a new scoreboard intentionally.

That scoreboard might include:

- Peace of mind
- Progress toward long-term goals
- Control over your time
- Consistency in habits

- Reduced stress around money
- Alignment between work and life

In tennis terms, this is deciding how you want to win points before the match starts.

When you define success clearly, decisions get easier. You spend with purpose. Save with confidence. Say no without guilt. Comparison loses its grip.

The Investing Concept Explained Through Tennis

Tennis teaches patience.

You do not win matches by hitting winners on every ball. You win by constructing points, managing risk, and trusting your game over time.

Financial success works the same way.

Chasing status is like chasing winners. It looks impressive but leads to errors. Chasing performance is like playing percentage tennis. It feels boring, but it wins.

Your financial life should support how you want to live, not how you want to be seen.

Coach's Perspective: What Would Your Coach Say?

A coach would reframe the conversation.

"Define how you want to win."

"Stop playing to the crowd."

"Trust your game."

"Play the long match."

"Do not beat yourself."

"Process over results."

Great coaches know that confidence comes from preparation, not applause.

Game Situations and Decision Points

Situation One:

You see a former teammate posting their new lifestyle. Do you compare, or do you stay focused on your plan?

That mirrors staying patient when the opponent goes for flashy shots.

Situation Two:

You hit an income milestone. Do you ask what matters next, or do you chase the next visible upgrade?

That mirrors resetting your strategy after winning a set.

Situation Three:

You feel pressure to look successful. Do you build alignment or buy validation?

That mirrors choosing shot selection under pressure.

The scoreboard you choose determines how you play.

Common Athlete Mistakes and Financial Parallels

Athletes chase validation.

Financially, that leads to overspending.

Athletes avoid introspection.

Financially, that leads to misaligned goals.

Athletes confuse winning with visibility.

Financially, that leads to regret.

Athletes abandon their game plan under pressure.

Financially, that leads to inconsistency.

Winning the Long Game

Redefining winning is not lowering standards.

It is raising them.

When success aligns with who you are and how you want to live, discipline becomes easier. Decisions feel lighter. The pressure to prove yourself fades.

You stop chasing highlights and start winning matches.

Athlete Takeaways

- Status is not the same as winning
- Income supports fulfillment, it does not replace it
- Comparison leads to forced errors
- Success evolves with life stages
- Build a scoreboard that matches your game

Chapter 30: Staying Connected Without Living in the Past

Think about the stretch of a tennis season when tournaments stack up.

You are traveling constantly. Different cities. Different courts. Different opponents. What keeps you steady is not just your forehand or fitness. It is the people around you. Coaches. Training partners. Physios. Teammates back home checking in. The routine of showing up to the same faces who know your game, your habits, and your mindset.

Then the season ends.

Eventually, the matches stop altogether.

For many former tennis players, the biggest loss after leaving the sport is not competition. It is connection. The locker room disappears. The daily rhythm of shared struggle fades. What used to be a built-in community becomes silence unless you intentionally replace it.

Staying connected matters. But living in the past does not.

The Role of Community, Mentorship, and New Locker Rooms

Tennis may be an individual sport, but no one succeeds alone.

Behind every player is a team. Coaches. Trainers. Hitting partners. Teammates from college or academies. People who push you, challenge you, and hold you accountable.

After tennis, that structure vanishes quickly.

If you do not replace it, isolation fills the gap.

New locker rooms exist, but they look different. Work teams. Professional organizations. Business partners. Community groups. Volunteer boards. Faith communities. Alumni networks. Peer groups of former athletes.

Mentorship matters too.

Learning from someone a few steps ahead saves time, money, and emotional energy. In tennis terms, this is having a coach who has already played on the courts you are stepping onto.

Community is not about nostalgia. It is about momentum.

Why Isolation Hits Former Athletes Hard

Isolation is dangerous because it is quiet.

There is no whistle. No warning shot. No dramatic collapse.

Former athletes go from constant interaction to independent schedules almost overnight. No teammates in the locker room. No shared practices. No post-match debriefs. Even successful careers can feel lonely when connection disappears.

In tennis terms, this is playing a long match without communication from your box. No feedback. No reminders. No emotional regulation.

Mistakes multiply when no one is watching.

Isolation often shows up as overwork, disengagement, anxiety, or withdrawal. People stay busy but feel disconnected. They mistake independence for strength while losing perspective.

Connection provides calibration. Without it, decision-making drifts.

Finding Purpose Without the Team

One of the hardest truths after tennis is this.

The team does not come back.

Purpose has to evolve.

Many former players chase the exact feeling tennis gave them. The adrenaline. The clarity. The applause. When they cannot find it, they feel restless or stuck.

In tennis terms, this is refusing to adjust your game as conditions change. Same swing. Same tactics. Different opponent. Different court.

Purpose after sports comes from impact, not applause.

Teaching. Leading. Building. Mentoring. Creating. Supporting others. Competing against yourself instead of opponents.

The competitive drive does not disappear. It just needs a new outlet.

Former athletes who thrive redirect that energy instead of replaying old matches.

Healthy Nostalgia vs Being Stuck

Remembering your playing days is healthy.

Living there is not.

Healthy nostalgia honors what tennis gave you. Discipline. Confidence. Work ethic. Resilience. It informs who you are today without defining who you must remain.

Being stuck shows up subtly.

Every story starts with what you used to do. Every comparison goes back to your ranking, your wins, your best match. Identity stops evolving.

In tennis terms, this is watching old match film instead of preparing for the next opponent.

The past should be a foundation, not a destination.

Creating a Forward-Looking Identity

Identity must move forward.

You are not a tennis player who used to play. You are a person who learned how to prepare, compete, adjust, and endure through tennis.

Those skills still matter.

In tennis terms, this is transferring fundamentals to a new surface. The court changes. The strokes still work.

A forward-looking identity asks better questions:

- Who am I becoming now?
- What skills do I want to develop next?
- Where do I want to contribute?
- Who do I want in my corner?

When identity evolves, connection follows naturally. You seek people aligned with who you are becoming, not who you were.

The Investing Concept Explained Through Tennis

Long-term financial success depends on connection as much as discipline.

Advisors. Mentors. Accountability partners. Trusted peers. These relationships protect you from blind spots and emotional decisions.

Trying to manage everything alone increases risk.

In tennis terms, this is firing your coach mid-match and deciding to wing it. You might survive for a while. Eventually, mistakes pile up.

Community keeps you grounded. Mentorship shortens learning curves. Accountability sustains habits when motivation fades.

Coach's Perspective: What Would Your Coach Say?

A coach would challenge you directly.

"Stop isolating."

"You don't train alone for a reason."

"Find your people."

"Honor the past, but prepare for what's next."

"Stay coachable."

"Keep growing."

Great coaches know stagnation is more dangerous than failure.

Game Situations and Decision Points

Situation One:

You feel disconnected after leaving tennis. Do you isolate further, or do you intentionally build new community?

That mirrors choosing whether to engage or drift during a long rally.

Situation Two:

You miss the team environment. Do you relive the past, or do you create a new locker room?

That mirrors adjusting tactics when conditions change.

Situation Three:

You define yourself by what you used to be. Do you evolve, or do you stay comfortable?

That mirrors refusing to adapt your game.

Connection shapes identity. Identity shapes decisions.

Common Athlete Mistakes and Financial Parallels

Athletes cling to past identity.

Financially, that leads to stagnation.

Athletes isolate.

Financially, that leads to poor decisions.

Athletes avoid change.

Financially, that limits opportunity.

Athletes wait for the old structure to return.

Financially, that delays progress.

Winning the Long Game

Staying connected does not mean staying the same.

The most successful former athletes build new communities, seek mentorship, and redefine purpose without erasing their past.

They treat life like a long match, not a highlight reel.

The game continues. Just on a different court.

Athlete Takeaways

- Tennis was a chapter, not the whole story
- Isolation increases mistakes
- Community and mentorship protect progress
- Honor the past without living there
- Build a forward-looking identity and keep playing

Glossary of Tennis and Financial Terms

This glossary connects key financial concepts to familiar ideas from **tennis**, making money easier to understand through the language, structure, and discipline players already know.

Asset Allocation

Financial Definition:

How money is divided among different investment types such as stocks, bonds, and cash to balance risk and return.

Tennis Comparison:

Court positioning and shot selection. If you camp the baseline and never come forward, or rush the net without preparation, you become predictable and unstable. Balance creates consistency.

Assets

Financial Definition:

Things you own that have value, such as cash, investments, real estate, or retirement accounts.

Tennis Comparison:

Your strengths as a player. Technique, fitness, experience, mental toughness, and preparation that contribute to winning matches.

Bonds

Financial Definition:

Loans made to governments or companies that pay interest and return principal over time.

Tennis Comparison:

High-percentage rally balls. Not flashy winners, but they keep you in the point and steady when pressure rises.

Budget

Financial Definition:

A plan for how income is allocated toward expenses, savings, and goals.

Tennis Comparison:

Match strategy. Without a plan for point construction, errors pile up and momentum disappears.

Cash Flow

Financial Definition:

Money coming in versus money going out.

Tennis Comparison:

Energy management over a match. Go too hard early and you fade late.

Compounding

Financial Definition:

Earnings that generate additional earnings over time.

Tennis Comparison:

Daily drills and repetition. Each session builds skill so improvement accelerates instead of restarting from scratch.

Credit

Financial Definition:

The ability to borrow money with the promise of repayment.

Tennis Comparison:

Trust with officials and opponents. Earned through consistency, lost quickly through poor behavior.

Debt

Financial Definition:

Money borrowed that must be repaid, often with interest.

Tennis Comparison:

Unforced errors. A few may be manageable, but too many cost matches.

Diversification

Financial Definition:

Spreading investments across different assets to reduce risk.

Tennis Comparison:

Having more than one weapon. Relying only on a forehand makes you easy to defend.

Emergency Fund

Financial Definition:

Savings set aside for unexpected expenses.

Tennis Comparison:

A medical timeout or extra stringing. You hope you never need it, but it keeps small issues from ending the match.

ETF (Exchange-Traded Fund)

Financial Definition:

A fund that holds many investments and trades like a stock.

Tennis Comparison:

Doubles play. Shared responsibility reduces pressure on any one player.

Fees / Expense Ratios

Financial Definition:

Costs associated with managing investments.

Tennis Comparison:

Poor footwork or lazy recovery. Small inefficiencies that quietly cost points over time.

Growth Investing

Financial Definition:

Investing in companies expected to grow faster than average.

Tennis Comparison:

Aggressive shot selection. Higher upside, but mistakes are punished without strong fundamentals.

Insurance

Financial Definition:

Protection against financial loss from unexpected events.

Tennis Comparison:

Protective gear and recovery protocols. You do not step on court without managing risk.

Liquidity

Financial Definition:

How easily money can be accessed without penalty or delay.

Tennis Comparison:

Court movement. The ability to adjust quickly when the rally changes.

Net Worth

Financial Definition:

Assets minus liabilities.

Tennis Comparison:

Match score, not one highlight. The total outcome matters more than any single point.

Rebalancing

Financial Definition:

Adjusting investments back to their intended mix over time.

Tennis Comparison:

Tactical adjustments mid-match to restore balance and control.

Risk

Financial Definition:

The chance that outcomes differ from expectations, including loss.

Tennis Comparison:

Shot difficulty. The higher the risk, the higher the potential reward.

Roth IRA

Financial Definition:

A retirement account where money grows tax-free if rules are followed.

Tennis Comparison:

Putting in extra conditioning early so the later sets feel easier.

Stocks

Financial Definition:

Ownership shares in a company.

Tennis Comparison:

Primary weapons. They drive scoring but need consistency and support.

Tax-Advantaged Accounts

Financial Definition:

Accounts that provide tax benefits, often with rules and restrictions.

Tennis Comparison:

Structured training programs. Rules exist to improve long-term results.

Volatility

Financial Definition:

Short-term ups and downs in market value.

Tennis Comparison:

Momentum swings. Normal unless you panic and abandon your plan.

Permanent Loss

Financial Definition:

Money that cannot recover due to poor decisions or panic.

Tennis Comparison:

A match-ending injury or collapse caused by ignoring fundamentals.

Total Return

Financial Definition:

Investment return from both price growth and income.

Tennis Comparison:

Winning the match, not just flashy points. Every part counts.

Value Investing

Financial Definition:

Investing in assets believed to be undervalued.

Tennis Comparison:

Solid percentage tennis. Less flash, more control, consistent results.

Yield

Financial Definition:

Income generated from an investment.

Tennis Comparison:

Reliable point construction. Not spectacular, but dependable.

Final Note

This glossary reinforces one core principle:

Financial success, like success in **tennis**, comes from balance, discipline, timing, and repetition.

That philosophy runs through **Tennis Money 101** and well beyond the final match.

Disclaimers

Educational Purpose Only

This book is for educational purposes only.

The information provided in **Tennis Money 101** is intended to help readers understand general financial concepts using **tennis-based analogies**. It is not individualized financial, investment, tax, legal, or insurance advice.

Every financial situation is different. Your goals, income, family circumstances, risk tolerance, and time horizon are unique. What works for one person may not be appropriate for another.

Not Financial, Investment, or Legal Advice

Nothing in this book should be interpreted as a recommendation to buy, sell, or hold any specific investment, financial product, or strategy.

This book does not replace advice from qualified professionals such as:

- Financial advisors
- Accountants or tax professionals
- Attorneys
- Insurance professionals

Before making financial decisions, readers should consult professionals who can evaluate their individual situation.

No Guarantees or Promises of Results

All investing involves risk, including the possible loss of principal.

Past performance does not guarantee future results. Markets fluctuate. Economic conditions change. Outcomes cannot be predicted or guaranteed.

The examples and scenarios in this book are illustrative only and may not reflect actual results or real-world outcomes.

Tax and Legal Information

Any discussion of taxes, retirement accounts, estate planning, or legal structures is general in nature.

Tax laws and regulations change frequently and vary by jurisdiction. Legal requirements differ based on location and personal circumstances. Readers should seek personalized tax or legal advice before acting on any information related to these topics.

Athlete and Career Considerations

This book discusses financial topics as they relate to athletes and former athletes, including career transitions and income changes.

It does not provide career placement services, employment advice, or guarantees related to income, compensation, or career success.

Use of Analogies

Tennis and sports analogies are used to make financial concepts easier to understand.

These analogies are educational tools only and should not be interpreted literally. Financial decisions require analysis beyond analogy.

Personal Responsibility

By reading this book, you acknowledge that:

- You are responsible for your own financial decisions
- You understand that financial outcomes involve uncertainty
- You agree to seek appropriate professional guidance when needed

Education improves decision-making, but responsibility remains with the individual.

Contact Information

If you would like to learn more about the concepts discussed in this book or explore additional educational resources, Pat Brown can be found through public platforms including LinkedIn, Twitter, and via Google search.

For questions specifically related to **Tennis Money 101**, you may contact Pat Brown at:

info@tennismoney101.com

Final Reminder

Financial success is built over time through discipline, planning, and consistency.

This book provides a framework, not a guarantee.

Use it as a guide, not a substitute for professional advice.

Pat Brown OLB, University of Kansas